The Soul Map

Seven Divine Levels of Spiritual Evolution

Paige Bartholomew

Love Revolution Publishing
Austin, Texas

Editors
Judy Leecraft
Angela Poorman

Cover Art
Judy Leecraft
Paige Bartholomew

Illustrations: Fair Use

Love Revolution Publishing
Austin, Texas

PAIGE BARTHOLOMEW

This book and all the love poured into it
Is dedicated to
Earth's Awakening Humans.
You Know Who You Are.

Special Thanks and Love to:

Quinn Bohlmann
Hayden Bohlmann
Judy Leecraft

PAIGE BARTHOLOMEW

Table of Contents

The Reason You Picked Up This Book
Introduction: My Life and Path to this Work

The Reason You Picked Up This Book

Deep inside your soul, there are memories which tell of a wondrous time on Earth: a time which has been foretold for millennia by ancient sages and saints. It is a time when all the eyes of the galaxy are on us. You may sense a coming transformation so big that you cannot fathom what might show up. You may feel a deep, upwelling feeling of yearning for something ineffable... You may sense a powerful urge toward some huge purpose, yet you may not know for what, just yet. You may feel an inner wail, a deep sorrow for humanity, and an unrelenting desire to help.

The Soul Map will help you make sense of all of this. It will help you remember Who You Are. It will help you discern your soul's developmental station and that of others you care for. With this information, you'll be better equipped to manage your relationships by understanding how your station matches or mismatches with those of your lover, parents, children, friends or co-workers. It will guide you toward intuiting how to have healthier relationships with everyone. This book will help you catch a glimpse of where you're headed next - as a mighty SOUL of the Universe! It will shed light on what humanity is encountering at this very moment.

There are many developmental psychology books written by mental health professionals. Likewise, there are many spiritual and self-help books written by mystics. Here, we'll do something new. This is a book written by a mental health professional who also happens to be a mystic. **It is an attempt to compare and contrast the way your human psyche develops with the way your soul develops. The stages are surprisingly similar.** If you know the human self, inside and out, you

i

know the soul-self. By the end of this book, you'll be able to read the map of your own soul.

My Path to This Work

Austin, Texas is a liberal and creative city. There are hippies and hipsters, musicians and artists, healers, therapists and writers everywhere. I was born and raised in Austin Texas. I still live here. If I were going to choose a place to be born, Austin was as good a choice as any for a mystic like me. However, not all Austinites are awakening. I was born into Austin society back in the 1970's, which was a group far from self-aware. My first challenge in life would be trying to fit in to a social world that didn't match my essential frequency.

My father was a successful business-man and my mother was a sorority gal who was into the ladies' Junior League. There are four of us kids. We went to private schools. We were homecoming kings, football and baseball stars, cheerleaders and members of high falutin' sororities and fraternities. Figuring out that I was a mystic growing up in a family like mine, in a well-to-do social circle, meant a lifetime of hiding my true self. I had to do it to survive. I had to hide if I didn't want to get shamed, ridiculed, outcast, or have my soul-light snuffed out. I learned not to be myself because I felt ashamed.

Growing up in this world is hard for most people. It's true. I don't make any claims that my problems were tougher than anyone else's, because all hardship is hard - and everything is relative.

My parents divorced when I was 13. I was separated from my siblings at the age of 14 and was forced to grow up without them. I realize that it might be disrespectful to my living relatives to publicly speak about specific details of family events of that time - so I'll keep things in "I" messages and talk only about my own experience and feelings. Let's suffice it to say that the tragedies that came to pass during those years shattered my family to a degree that has not yet been possible to repair.

In my young home-life, I felt like an alien. I experienced rejection, judgment and betrayal from the people I loved and trusted the most. I spent my formative years confused and very, very sad. What happened to me broke me into a thousand little pieces. It's taken my entire adult life to collect all of those little pieces and glue them back together in a way that looks something like a human being again.

I was extraordinarily sensitive from the start. My father said I was "too sensitive" - whatever that means. My clothes felt unbearably itchy, abrupt noises shocked my system, smells made me sick (smells that other people often couldn't detect.) Some activities were so overstimulating they sent me into frenzied panic. The emotional turmoil of the household crashed over me incessantly like ocean waves, crushing me under an invisible weight, a weight that others didn't seem to notice as acutely as I did. I complained about my discomfort. I was a child who was extremely uncomfortable in my own body and I needed help. Children in need naturally cry out. That seemed to be a problem for my family. I got the message that I was my father's greatest irritation. I never did get the help I so desperately needed. Instead I got labeled the bad one, the crazy one, and the black sheep.

I remember so many lonely weekends, when there was nothing to do, feeling so depressed and lonely I could barely manage it. And there was another unexplainable feeling, too: homesickness. I never understood how I could feel homesick while I was wandering around my own home. It was much later that I came to realize what I was truly homesick for.

Many years into my adulthood, I read an article on living in the world as an empath. Learning what that term meant explained so much about who I am and soothed my confused mind. (We'll explore the phenomenon of the empath more deeply throughout this book). Finally, the sensitivities I was born with began to make more sense - which was a huge relief.

"What's an Empath," You Ask?

An Empath is a person who is extraordinarily sensitive to the emotions of other people. Another good descriptor of this type of human might be the term, "emotionally psychic". An empath can sense other people's emotions, even those a person may not be aware they are feeling. An empath may be able to sense another's emotional state before the person has entered the room. Not only do empaths sense other people's emotions, but they often take them on and IN. Empaths are highly skilled energy workers. (Yes, even when they are unaware of it, and still untrained. They're born like this naturally.) They instinctively, and often unconsciously, draw others' emotions into their body, filter it, and then send it back out... changed. Empaths who have spent their lives doing their own work to heal past wounds can become highly skilled therapists and healers. Before I was old enough to do my personal work, before I became consciously integrated enough to become a therapist, I was a child naturally processing the energy of a very toxic family. I was a child who was drowning in her family's toxic waste.

It took many, many years to wade through the chaos, confusion, and excruciating grief of my past. It took years of therapy to figure out the truth about my family's dysfunction and how I played into it. It took years of spiritual study and practice to realize that I am an intuitive empath, and to hone those innate gifts into something I could understand and control. I made it my life's work to overcome the traumas that occurred within my family of origin. From my many years of working with clients with complex PTSD, I have come to believe that it is very rare for 3D humans to ever fully recover from trauma. I still work on it every day of my life. Finding the courage to do my work is something I am most proud of. Regularly attending therapy and other groups, or engaging in various forms of self-exploration is something to be proud of. Healing and understanding myself and the people I love is my passion and my driving force in life.

The Weird Stuff Begins

As a very young person, I began experiencing memories of other lives, in other worlds. I didn't have the language to explain what I was experiencing or why those memories made me feel so homesick. It was only later in life that I was able to build a context for them.

In 1998, I found Sufism and began studying the 28 stations of the Sufi path. My guide, Sidi Muhammad Al-Jamal Ash-Shadhuli taught me how to clean up my lower self and how to open to my higher self. Through his teachings, I was able to understand the true nature of my own soul. I was able to see who I really am. This was the greatest gift Sidi gave me. I came to understand that I was not only an "empath", but a "mystic." A mystic is a person who seeks for union with a divine being, who longs for understanding of universal mystery, cosmology and the evolution of the human soul. She spends time contemplating unity in an attempt to become immersed into the Absolute. She believes in truths that exist behind what the eyes can see, and the mind can comprehend.

After beginning to study Sufism I became intensely interested in the topic of soul evolution. I wanted to know the process by which a soul grows and evolves. No, I wanted to remember it. I was obsessed with it.

Many of the concepts in this book have been inspired by Sidi's teachings. His presence in my life catalyzed my own deep, hidden knowledges of ancient truths.

I'm not a psychic. I'm not a channel. I wasn't told the information presented in this book from some other being. I didn't read it. I remember it.

There's a distinct difference between learning something new and remembering something you have temporarily forgotten. When one is presented with a brand new concept, they first feel confused. It takes a lot of time and practice to let the information settle in the brain and create new neural pathways... new soul pathways.

Remembering concepts is different. Remembering feels like recognition. Remembering is effortless. It ignites a sense of inspiration, excitement, and joy! Sometimes it comes with tingles all over. I never felt like I learned this material. It always felt like I was rediscovering lost memories from another place and time.

When we are born and we get our Earth suit, it comes with a veil of amnesia that makes us forget everything that happened before our birth. We all have ancient memories stored deep within us from other lives in more primitive levels of consciousness, and those memories can be accessed. I happen to be one who was born with many of my soul memories intact. It was through deep prayer, meditation, spiritual study, and spiritual practice that I was able to put those ancient feelings and images into a context my mind could grasp, and that I might someday be able to teach. My studies served as catalysts to remind me of what I already innately knew.

I am blessed to have been guided by some of the wisest, holiest spiritual teachers on the planet today. I also consider myself blessed to have been escorted by unseen teachers in spirit, as well as by my own secret place within my heart.

I have memories of living in other realms, other worlds, in other times. I have memories of breathtaking realities in very high levels of being. The material I will present here is an amalgamation of some of the material I have learned through study, combined with many of my soul memories.

Some of the information you'll find in this book may sound a lot like things you've studied elsewhere. In part, that's probably because you and I have trained in similar paths. We've all read the same books, listened to the same podcasts, and seen the same speakers. As I discovered new texts and documents through the years, there was a sense of validation for me as if I already knew the material. A Course in Miracles, The Law of One, the work of David Hawkins, and so many other brilliant visionaries served to awaken my own innate memories of cosmic wisdom. Buddhism, Vedanta, Sufism, Christianity, Native American Shamanism; there are whispers of them all within these pages.

Upon reading many of these sources over the years, it was a great surprise to me to find that there was a feeling of unearthing something ancient. For me, reading certain texts causes a flood of downloads. Information rushes in all at once. I'm aware that these filmy whispers, visions, and veiled knowings have been there since I was a small child.

Much of the material you will read here came from my own meditations and are not from communications with another entity, but from my own higher self, remembering what I learned about Reality from many lifetimes.

Truth is Truth. Jesus, Buddha, Muhammad, Ra, Tolle, Chopra... they reported the truth as they remembered it from their own inner knowing. This is what I'm doing. There's no corner on the market for Universal Truth. It cannot be patented or copy-righted. It's everywhere; in everyone. So, if some of my material sounds similar, well, the Universe has a way of sending important information to us in repeating waves. It is God's way of making sure we get the point.

So now, I open my heart to you. I offer what I am able, to help you open your own ancient soul memories. I am but one person, living in a vast universe absolutely FILLED with sparks of the Divine. It's my intention to share the Grand System with you as I remember it. You may not agree with what I present here. That's ok. I want you to believe what you believe in your own way, and to find YOUR Truth in your own time. If anything I say helps you on your path, then I give credit to the Divine for that, for it is the Divine who taught me.

I love you in the places where your family rejected you. I see your beauty in the places where society sees only "strange." I give you space to explore yourself in whatever way serves you best. I'm interested in your journey. You are a gift to this world. You are God's PRIZED POSSESSION. You CAN heal from your past. You can transcend this base world. You can arise to live in the station of your soul - the person you truly are. Let's do it together.

Love, Paige

PAIGE BARTHOLOMEW

~ SECTION ONE ~

The Basics of the Path

Chapter 1

The Chakra Map

Chakras Are Your GPS System

Hidden within your body is an energetic template that holds all the information your soul needs for its journey back to Source. It's called your chakra system. Through studying the system of chakras and the information embedded inside each one, you can approach a better understanding of the stages of soul development.

Think of your chakra system not only as a set of energy centers in the body, but as a map for your soul's evolution. Each chakra contains a complete curriculum within it. Each chakra represents a developmental soul stage. Each chakra holds a different set of developmental lessons for your being to learn. Understanding the curriculum of each chakra will give you a keen understanding of human behavior, and also true spirituality.

There is much information on the internet about chakras which you can investigate for yourself, but here, I'll I give a simple breakdown of the main themes for each one:

The first chakra: "I am." In this stage of development, we learn the lessons of physical being-ness. "I exist." The first chakra is located at the base of the spine and vibrates at the frequency of the color red.

The second chakra: "I feel/I want." In this stage of development, we become conscious of our self and our relationship to others. We learn about emotions, our survival instincts and reproduction. "I'm aware that I exist, and I'm aware that I need the support of my clan to survive. Whether they accept me leads to life or death." The second chakra is located just below the navel and vibrates at the frequency of the color orange.

The third chakra: "I can." In this stage of development, we master personal power. The intellect prevails. "I can create, manipulate, do, have, and act by using my will. My own needs and desires are at the forefront of my consciousness and I'll do

2

whatever I can to meet them." The third chakra is located just below the sternum and vibrates at the frequency of the color yellow.

The fourth chakra: "I love." In this stage of development, we learn to balance the lower three chakras through love. We learn to live in compassion and acceptance of all beings. We learn that Love heals. "Others' needs matter as much as mine do. I realize that to hurt another is to hurt myself. I care for all of creation." Extreme empathy, rudimentary telepathic ability, and some extra-sensory perceptions appear at this level. The fourth chakra is located in the middle of the chest and vibrates at the frequency of the color green.

The fifth chakra: "I know truth." In this stage of development, we learn what it feels like to *merge* with all beings. We realize our multidimensional existence. "I experience myself as existing on many levels at once. I can finally discern truth vs. falsehood with perfect acuity." The fifth chakra is located in the throat and vibrates at the frequency of the color blue.

The sixth chakra: "I am one with the *creation*." In this stage of development, we come to know that there are no separate parts in all the multiverse. The heart and intellect become perfectly balanced. Merging with others while keeping a boundaried self is realized. We gain insight into the eternal, fractal-like nature of the creation. We experience everything as one being. "I am all that is. I am all of creation. There is no separation between anything. It's all just one thing." The sixth chakra is located between the eyebrows, in the middle of the brain, and vibrates at the frequency of the color sapphire.

The seventh chakra: "I am one with the *Creator*." In this stage of development, understanding surpasses the created realms and moves into eternal knowledge. It cannot be understood with the mind. "I am all that is and all that is not. God and I are not separate." The seventh chakra is located at the crown of the head and vibrates at the frequency of the color violet.

Colors of the Visual Rainbow

The colors of the rainbow are a nice way to conceptualize your soul's levels of consciousness. White light can be broken down through a prism to reveal seven distinct colors. Photons which show as the color red have the longest wavelength and travel at the slowest rate of speed. As photons speed up, they appear to change color from red, to orange, to yellow, to green, to blue, to sapphire, to violet. Photons appearing as the color violet travel via the shortest wavelength and move at the fastest rate of speed.

Color	Wavelength	Frequency	Photon Energy
Violet	380 – 450 nm	668 – 789 THz	2.90 – 3.26 eV
Sapphire	450 - 425 nm	670 - 700 Thz	2.70 – 2.90 eV
Blue	450 – 495 nm	606 –668 THz	2.50 – 2.70 eV
Green	495 – 570 nm	526 – 606 THz	2.17 – 2.50 eV
Yellow	570 – 590 nm	508 – 526 THz	2.10 – 2.17 eV
Orange	590 – 620 nm	484 – 508 THz	2.00 – 2.10 eV
Red	620 – 750 nm	400 – 484 THz	1.60 – 2.00 eV

The seven colors of the rainbow can be likened to the seven stages of soul development. Red ray corresponds to the first stage of soul development. Orange ray corresponds to the second stage of soul development, and so on. All of the colors of the rainbow are encompassed within White Light, just as all of the seven stages of consciousness are encompassed within the One All-Knowing Creator.

Notes of the Musical Scale

Just like color travels through space as a wavelength, so does sound. The seven chakras correspond not only to the seven colors of the visible rainbow, but also to the seven notes on a musical scale.

Note	Frequency (Hz)	Wavelength (cm)
B	30.87	1117.67
A	27.50	1254.55
G	24.50	1408.18
F	21.83	1580.63
E	20.60	1674.62
D	18.35	1879.69
C	16.35	2109.89

Each note on the scale can be correlated to each of the seven stages of soul development. Color repeats in a spiraling pattern upward into higher and higher frequencies -- from infra-red to ultra-violet and beyond. Sound does the same thing. Musical notes rise incrementally in higher and higher octaves (frequencies) of sound, up into ranges such as the high pitches that animals can hear. Sound and color fractalize both upwards and downwards in hertz - INFINTELY. Science hasn't yet proven this, but according to the Laws of the One Creator, it's probable that all energy moves in an infinite spiraling pattern.

Spiritual growth fractalizes infinitely as well. Once we grow through the seven stages of soul development, we reach the top end of this known reality, and finally arrive at the "octave" (just like notes on a musical scale). In this book, we'll stop at the level of the octave (the gateway at the end of Seventh Density), but rest assured - there is more mystery thereafter.

Do Time and Space Have an End?

Time and Space are creations. So are color and light. All created things are finite. Since only the Creator is Infinite, it makes sense that at a certain point, all time and space, color and light will collapse into a singularity (imagine a black hole). A singularity is a place where everything which has been created ceases to exist, but where all original intelligence exists eternally. This singularity is what we call *infinity.*

Where we go beyond the octave, we will only know when we arrive! How wondrous will that be?

What is Real?

Sometimes we tend to think that which is physical is real, and that which is non-physical is imaginary. We tend to make a split between physicality and energy, when the fact is, both are the same thing. Everything in this 3D world that you live in is made up of the One Essence. Take a look deeper than cells, atoms, quarks, or even dark matter. What's behind the physics? **Everything, even energy, is made up of *consciousness.***

Your soul is pure consciousness. Everything you experience, from the inception of your soul, through every world you'll ever live in is created by your consciousness. **Physicality is only one projection of your consciousness.** Your life purpose here is to grow in consciousness. The concept that **consciousness creates all of the worlds** is going to be very important as you move along in this body of work.

Evolutionary Soul Levels

Each chakra in your body contains within it a map that holds all the vital information you need to navigate your path of spiritual evolution. These are the seven major levels through which you travel on your way to enlightenment. One level leads to the next, as you take everything you learned with you to the following stage. Each position is like a newly upgraded operating system. Every soul level is a complete world or realm unto itself. One term I think describes these soul levels really well, is **"densities".** The Law of One material (Elkins, 1984) also uses this term when they describe the phenomenon of multiple, ascending realms.

There is a difference between a density and a dimension. Currently on Earth, we have 3 dimensions of space, and 1 dimension of time. Conversely, a density is a self-contained section of space/time. It is a realm of consciousness, created collectively by sentient beings. Each density is a distinct kingdom which vibrates within its own specific band of energy frequency.

In George Van Tassel's book, *The Council of 7 Lights,* he distinguishes between densities and dimensions. He writes, "Do not confuse densities with dimensions. **Densities** are pressures, established in charging frequencies of vibration (like a pressurized bubble). **Dimensions** are measurements..." (Van Tassel, 1999). I will be using the word "densities" interchangeably with "levels" throughout the book.

Many spiritual people have gotten used to the idea that humanity will be shifting from the third dimension directly to the fifth dimension. If you think about it, how and why would a species skip a whole step in their evolution? Some person used the term "fifth dimension" at some point and it caught on. In my model, we are not skipping from 3D to 5D. It's not possible to do so. Humanity has to take the route of the third level to the fourth, and that's where we're going: the fourth level.

Many people discuss the Great Shift in terms of humanity moving from the third dimension to the fifth dimension. If you think about it, how and why would a species skip a whole step in evolution? Some person used the term, "fifth dimension" at some point and it caught on. In my model, we are not skipping from 3D to 5D. It's not possible to do so. Humanity has to take the route of the third level to the fourth, and that's where we're going: the fourth level.

It's not possible to perceive things that exist in frequency bands outside of your own. If you live in Third Density, you cannot see into Fourth Density, etc. There are worlds upon worlds lying one on top of the next... or you could think of them as existing one INSIDE the other! Imagine densities as Russian nesting dolls. Each one literally resides within the rest. Once you cross through to a new soul level, you can see the previous ones that you traversed before. Each successive realm grows more extraordinarily complex and beautiful than the last.

Every level, or density, holds its own unique opportunities for learning. Each developmental stage of your spiritual growth builds on what was learned in the last one. Souls evolve by traversing these densities one at a time. It takes many thousands of lifetimes and eons of time to go from start to finish.

Our chakra system has given us a map to follow. It has given us a place to begin and a place to end, bookends with vast amounts of knowledge in between for us to study. It's as if the

Creator Itself has shown us exactly where it wants us to focus our attention: within these seven rays of soul development.

Chapter 2

The Seven Levels of Soul Evolution

Defining the Chakra Map

**"There are seven types of consciousness
that all humans will transform into:**

1. **Basic survival needs of life**
2. **Living by emotions**
3. **An urge to become super**
4. **Discover the secret key of love**
5. **Conscious use of consciousness**
6. **Direct connection to universal wisdom**
7. **Stationed permanently at the universal core"**

~ Bhushan Bhansali

We souls evolve in a predictable way. The map for the journey is written within our very DNA. *__The evolutionary map is the chakra system.__* If you understand the essential meanings and messages embedded within each chakra, you'll understand the evolutionary steps every soul takes on its way to remembering the truth of Who It Is. So, we will be studying each chakra and the curriculum it holds.

In the beginning, before time, each one of us was born from All-That-Is. It was then that we began our journeys through the levels of consciousness. Each chakra carries a set of lessons to learn. Mastering each one takes us to a new realm of consciousness to live in. Each realm is its own distinct paradigm or world. We graduate upwards along these realms as we develop. Each level is a schoolhouse specifically designed to teach the soul what it needs to know at every moment of its evolution.

The One from which you were created encoded your very soul with a map for you to follow. This Soul Map would guide you along your path back home. Home means reaching full enlightenment, where confusion has been fully worked through, and where you remember everything. The map is your greatest gift from God. When you learn how to use it through intuition and sensing, you can trust it to lead you exactly where you are supposed to go. Everything will begin to make sense for the first time. This map is the safe ship that will carry you across churning seas of the many created worlds, back home to the arms of your Beloved Creator.

The Stages of your Soul Map

The First Soul Level – Unconscious Existence

First Density is the introductory level of creation. All souls begin here. It's where you start your journey, freshly born from

All-That-Is. Here, you are in your most asleep state. The term, "asleep" doesn't imply "unconscious," but simply unaware. Beings living in First Density states are alive, but they're just not aware of themselves. First Density corresponds to the first chakra in the body, and the red light ray on the visible spectrum. In this first experience of life, you will exist as essential elements such as rock, air, water or fire.

The primary developmental milestone of this stage of growth is simply to **experience existence**.

The Second Soul Level – Physical Mastery

Second Density is the level where you have your first inkling of conscious awareness. Shifting from First Density to Second Density means a qualitative shift in your **experience of what it feels like to be alive.** Second Density corresponds to the second chakra in the body and the orange light ray on the visible spectrum. In this density you will exist as plant or animal - from protozoa to the most advanced mammal.

In Second Density, the primary developmental task of your soul is to develop a **conscious mastery of your physical form, your instincts and your emotions.**

The Third Soul Level – Self Empowerment

Third Density is the level at which you become human. Now you move into a body which possesses an upgraded brain with the ability for complex thought and verbal competencies. This is the level of consciousness at which your soul learns about who it is as an individual. Shifting from Second Density to Third Density means a qualitative change in your **understanding of your own personal nature.** Because it's really all about you in this level, we call it the station of the EGO. It's the home of the lower mind, more commonly called "the intellect." Third Density corresponds to the third chakra in the body and the yellow light ray on the visible spectrum.

The primary developmental task of the third level is **self-knowledge and self-empowerment**.

The Fourth Soul Level – The Illuminated Heart

Shifting from Third Density to Fourth Density means moving past your ego and making a qualitative change in your **understanding of love**. Humanity stands on the cusp of shifting into Fourth Density right now. In order to make the transition, you must purify your lower self and anchor yourself firmly in your heart. This is not the same love you felt in Third Density. This is true unconditional love, and will be felt, experienced, and expressed more richly than before.

It takes a lot of work to extract all the toxic debris from the collective ego-consciousness that humans have been carrying for eons. The good news is, Earth has already been doing this work for centuries. We're almost there! Many individuals have already made their personal shift and are living with Fourth Density consciousness now. When humanity reaches critical mass, those who are ready will follow suit, and the Earth itself will make her own shift. That's when we'll see a New World!

Fourth Density corresponds to the fourth chakra in the body and the green light ray on the visible spectrum. Once you make your personal shift into 4D, your body becomes much more sensitive and less dense. Food, sound, light, fragrance, emotions of others, or foreign energies may overwhelm you. You'll need to learn how to care for yourself in a whole new way.

The primary developmental task in the fourth level is to **master compassion equally for self and others.**

The Fifth Soul Level – The Illuminated Intellect

Shifting from Fourth Density to Fifth Density means making a qualitative change in **understanding your non-physical self.** Fifth Density is the home of the higher mind where *love and wisdom coalesce into complete conscious thought.* Until now, your awareness has been too muddied with lower chakra energies to access pure wisdom (yes, even in Fourth Density you were still largely unclear). You'll finally be able to combine everything you've learned from the lower four densities and merge it into a more complete understanding of who you are and what your existence is all about, physically, emotionally, mentally and spiritually.

Fifth Density corresponds to the fifth chakra in the body and the blue light ray on the visible spectrum. When you reach the point where you're ready to make your shift into Fifth Density consciousness, your body will tip the scales from matter into light. You will finally receive your light body! As the Earth makes its own shift into Fifth Density, it will change into an energetic world, and will no longer be dense. You'll be able to create what you need and want through the natural power of your being instead of through the clumsy use of technology.

The primary developmental task in the fifth level of consciousness is to **master the realm of wisdom.**

The Sixth Soul Level – Unity

Shifting from Fifth Density to Sixth Density means making a qualitative change in your **understanding of what it means to**

merge into oneness. At the sixth level, all knowledge will be combined between individuals so that a collective consciousness emerges. This is the first time that true recognition will be realized, for the self, for the other, and for all things everywhere: "good" and "bad." Everyone will be known as One Being. Trust between beings will be absolute here in Sixth Density. For the first time, negatively polarized individuals won't enter into or exist in this state of consciousness. They just can't tolerate the levels of light and truth that are required to live here. When recognition is realized and love is total – there's nowhere for negative entities to hide. They'll either slide backwards, or choose to change. It's as if polarity is absorbed into 'is-ness'. Polarity will dissolve.

Sixth Density corresponds to the sixth chakra in the body and the sapphire light ray on the visible spectrum. The primary developmental task is to master the realm of **cosmic knowledge.**

The Seventh Soul Level – The Threshold of Eternity

Shifting from Sixth Density to Seventh Density means making a qualitative change in your **understanding of creation itself, and Who You Are within THE ALL.** Understanding emerges about the way creation is made and the way it operates. You will comprehend the true nature of your relationship with the Creator. You will see the reasons for everything that happens in all the lower densities. In this station, all will become clear, but not to the mind as you know it. The human mind cannot process Seventh Density information, love and light. Here, understanding happens within the subtle spirit. This is the level at which "the many" merge back into "The One." Perfection is finally yours. No longer will you see yourself as a separate individual. No longer will you be working hard to clean and purify the lower parts of yourself. No longer will you struggle with pain and suffering. All of that is over. The learning here is very, very refined, silent, and stunning.

Seventh Density corresponds to the seventh chakra in the body and the violet light ray on the visible spectrum. The primary developmental task is to **remember Who You Always Were and to reunify with All That Is.**

Lifetimes

It takes thousands upon thousands of lifetimes to make our way through all the densities. Don't try to rush it. Don't pretend to be in a station you haven't achieved. It won't serve you. It's important to discern where you are, to accept it, and to learn to love the process. You can use The Soul Map to help you find your own level of consciousness. One level isn't better than another. Each density is a glorious world with so much beauty to enjoy and incredible interests to be inspired by - if you want to see them. It's up to you to make this journey beauty-full and awesome. **The first step to happiness in any level or state is to accept yourself where you are.** At the same time, never stop reaching for more learning. Striking a nice balance between the two will help you glide through your journey more smoothly.

Understanding your spiritual level, and the level of those around you, will give you a huge leg-up in figuring out why your relationships are the way they are. **The Soul Map will help explain why people behave the way they do, and it will help you see why you react the way you do in return**. Mastering this material will inform your choices about whom you choose to let into your heart, whom to trust, whom to safely learn from, and whom to let go of.

Mastering this model of evolution will make clear where you've been, where you are, and where you're going, just like a map.

Every minute of your life is an extra-ordinary opportunity for learning. It's easy to fall into a rut, to forget the truth, and become disillusioned. Take this moment to remember your true essence, the real being-ness of who you were created to be. Feel your heart within. It's a good heart! Know that just by reading these words on the page, your soul is begging you to WAKE UP! Your soul wants to LEARN and to LIVE FULLY! Take your chance now. State your intention before the Universe, your Creator, and all of the beings who support you. It's your time to remember everything about who you are, why you are here, and what you were always meant to be.

Chapter 3

The Way Your Soul Learns

Humans grow by a series of pulses. We surge forward, then rest on a plateau for a while, only to surge forward again. We can see this type of physical growth in children when they have growth spurts, gaining an inch or two seemingly overnight. We can see this pattern of emotional and psychological growth in developmental stages too, as people suddenly show a pronounced shift in *the way* they think. It is the same for spiritual growth. We souls make our way up the ladder of awakening one rung at a time, through a series of pulsed insights.

States and Stations

The Shadhuliyya Sufi Order uses specific terms to describe the way a soul evolves. According to my sheikh, humans experience "states" and "stations."

States

"States" are temporary thoughts or emotions. These states come in the form of belief systems (which are inherently unstable), opinions, changeable points of view, or your ever-evolving worldview. Sometimes states last a short time. For instance, in the case of being disappointed after missing a special occasion. Other states may last a very long time. An example being when one sustains a great loss which produces prolonged grief that colors her whole identity. The important thing to remember about states is that they are TRANSITORY, and not based on ultimate TRUTH.

There are Two Kinds of States

Peak States: You may have glimpses of a higher density from time to time. These are called *positive spiritual experiences,* or **peak states.**

Remember, states are impermanent experiences. Don't get discouraged if you reach a peak state and then it fades back into the "same-ole, same-ole." Their purpose is to give you yearning to reach higher. Let a peak spiritual experience teach you. Thank it for coming. But don't hold onto it. In trying to keep it, you may have a tendency to beat yourself up when it doesn't stick. **It's not supposed to stick.** Let it go and appreciate yourself as you are, here and now. You will get where you want to go! It's guaranteed.

Regressive States: There are moments in all of our lives when we temporarily regress backward emotionally or mentally. This is normal for all people, no matter how evolved. Here, in Third Density, it's common for events to trigger people into past memories of hurt, anger, fear, or trauma. We mustn't shame ourselves when we regress. Revolving in and out of pain or fear is the way we learn. It's your job to look at your feelings, accept them and to work with them in order to understand yourself better.

Remember, *it is impossible for your soul to go backwards*. And negative states don't stick forever either! States help us learn by giving us an opportunity to **feel our way through realities.**

Stations

According to Sheikh Sidi Al-Jamal, a soul reaches a new **station** when it crosses the boundary of limited perception into a new, **semi-permanent level of awareness.** Stations aren't the same as peak states. Crossing into a higher **station** means that you learned such a transformative lesson, it substantially changed the way you see yourself and reality.

States are fleeting, *illusory feelings* meant to help you learn.
Stations are semi-permanent *shifts in your perception.*
Levels/Densties are permanent changes in the *evolution of your SOUL.*

Current Working Models

We humans are given opportunities to create "working models" of our universe. These "working models" are semi-permanent **stations** which help you to conceptualize the world you live in, and the situations you're trying to work though. They last long enough to allow you to fully explore, and then grasp the lessons at hand, only to finally dissolve away, opening space for new models of belief to form.

You may have felt a peak experience or series of big insights that open your mind to new, expansive ideas. Elated -- you may have had the thought, "I finally have it all figured out"! The purpose is for you to run with your ideas, to take them to their limits, to apply the "working model" to your world in order to see everything through that lens. Eventually, the excitement drains away to something that feels more 'old hat,' as you plateau in your growth within the "model's" paradigm. Finally, the "working model" crumbles and you feel as if you don't know anything. Zip. Nothing makes sense. It can be quite confusing after such a period of certainty. Often, when a "working model" runs out of lessons for you, it can feel like a devastating, depressing, hopeless time, unless you understand what's happening, which you will after reading this. What's actually happened is that you've exhausted every possibility within that **station** of knowledge.

Soon, a new working model will arise, and you'll feel that same elation you did last time. Spiritual development feels good!

Learning what your being wants to learn is FUN! Soon, your zest for living and learning return and the cycle repeats itself. This process of pulsed-learning has been in effect since the birth of your soul. It's the process by which you learn everything there is to know in the universe. You go station by station through constantly upgrading prototypes.

Spiritual School

Consider the idea that moving upward in one's spiritual level is similar to the way kids move upward through grades in school. Do you remember third grade? During that year, you had lots of ups and downs. Those ups and downs were your **states**, which changed from day to day. Each homework assignment could be likened to a **state**. Remember, **states** change quickly as we learn.

Each time you finished a mathematics module, you stabilized in a whole new **station** of knowledge. Each academic module or chapter could be likened to a **station**. Remember that **stations** are longer-lasting, significant perceptual "working models" of understanding. You stayed in that math station until you learned it through and through. Then you were able to move on to higher levels of math lessons. Step after step, your insight broadened into "working models" about the way math works.

*Just because your emotional and mental **states** changed from day to day, doesn't mean your scholastic level changed.* You remained in the third grade until you mastered all the required material. Once you completed all the lessons at the end of the school year, you graduated to the fourth grade. Graduating from third grade to fourth grade is like shifting up in **density**. You learned everything a third grader can learn, and you'll never unlearn it. It's an everlasting change in you.

Illusion versus True Knowledge

An illusion is a misunderstanding or a mis-perception. Almost any 3D idea is an incomplete perception and not knowledge of the Truth.

True knowledge, or knowledge of the truth, produces a feeling of CERTAINTY. Each "working model" contains elements of True Knowledge within them, but they are not the Ultimate Truth. The closer we get to Fourth Density and above, clear insights become more frequent. Knowledge of the truth generally cannot be found in the lower intellectual mind in 3D. When you feel certainty you will recognize it. It carries a feeling of stability and impermeability. Your experience of True Knowledge may come with shivers or a sense that you are floating in timelessness. True Information arrives from your soul's storehouse of memories. It carries the essence of the Absolute.

"Mis-perceptions produce fear [regressive states].
True perceptions produce Love [peak states].
But neither produces certainty
because perceptions are variable.
That is why perception is not true knowledge.
Knowing is the affirmation of Truth.
Knowing is beyond all perception."
~ A Course in Miracles

Free-will Choice

You, as a soul, have control over how fast or how slow you evolve. It's within your power of choice to linger at a certain developmental level for many lifetimes - if that's what you desire. I bet you know someone who is completely grown, maybe in his forties or even fifties, who simply never grew up. For whatever reason, he was never ready to give up parts of his child-self. His adult behaviors still seem childlike or dysfunctional because of his choice to hold onto fantasies instead of continuing to accept True Reality.

It's the same with soul evolution. There are those who aren't ready to grow out of younger spiritual developmental stages. They may choose to camp out at certain dazzling tourist attractions without moving on, it may last for many, many lifetimes. This is completely permitted. God doesn't mind what we choose. There's no shame in it from "Heaven." Infinite Creator's first gift to creation was free-will. The fact is that you *will* eventually arrive at completion in the end, no matter how long you want to take to get there.

The book, *A Course in Miracles*, explains your soul's program of study this way: "This is a course in miracles. It is a required course. Only the time you take it is voluntary. Free-will does not mean that you can establish the curriculum. It means only that you can elect what you want to take at a given time. The course does not aim at teaching the meaning of love, for that is beyond what can be taught. It does aim, however, at removing the blocks to the awareness of love's presence, which is your natural inheritance" (Schucman, 2007).

When you're moving upward in evolution, those who aren't ready or willing to commit to impeccability won't be able to pass into the next density. This isn't meant as a punishment. If you want to hang out in Third Density for millennia — it's your decision to do so. And if you're ready to progress, **your yearning and your willingness will shine like a beacon, alerting the Universe that you are prepared for your next step.**

25

Your Emotional GPS System

Your soul learns through an amazing little system called *emotion.* **Turns out, those temporary emotional states are very useful!** (even though they aren't stable like stations, or permanent like densities.) Your feelings are like an instant bio-feedback mechanism constantly giving you messages. When you learn to use it properly, you'll be able to fully trust your emotional GPS system to guide you. Your higher self is always guiding you. It wants you to stay in alignment with it. When you're in alignment with your higher self, you feel good. When you are out of alignment with your higher self, you feel bad. It's pretty much that simple. Your higher self has an agenda for your learning and it wants you to stay the course. When you feel depressed, stuck, angry, sad, frustrated, anxious, or any other uncomfortable feeling, it is a direct sign that you're not on your true soul path.

More information about your emotional GPS system will be given in Section 2.

The Great Shift is HERE

Have patience! As I mentioned before, humanity is right on the cusp of making the transition from one permanent soul density to another. Open your heart. Let your yearning for God, Love, Kindness and Rightness sparkle brightly. Feel the fear and vulnerability and do the right thing anyway. The world needs YOU! It's about to get exciting around here!

Chapter 4

What's it like to Shift From One Level to the Next?

**This is the time of the Great Awakening.
The doors are opening to the next world. It takes a great deal of
energy for a soul to up-level.
When one is ready, it won't feel like work.
It will feel like bliss.**

Before we dive into great detail regarding the densities themselves, it's important to understand how the process of shifting between densities works. In between each level, there is an invisible veil: a **vibrational threshold**. The veil is like a one-way mirror. Those going toward the threshold perceive it like a mirror and cannot see through it. However, those who have already passed through to the other side can easily see back through to the density they left behind.

The veil is a gateway. In order to cross through the gateway between one density and the next, a soul must make fundamental changes within. These changes permanently raise your vibrational frequency. In order to pass through, you must _become_ the frequency of the gate. It's why many people are calling these years the time of **"The Great Shift."** A soul must literally _shift_ its vibrational frequency to be allowed access. The process of shifting your frequency cannot be rushed or forced. It's a natural process that unfolds because of your internal work, your intention and your yearning. Your job is simply to stretch open, to keep your heart honest, to stay aware of your shadows, to heal, learn, and to do your best to love in every situation. The river of life will do the rest. The key to moving through the densities is _willingness_. You don't have to know what to do!

"I learned to trust the Universe,
so the Universe chose to Trust me."
~ Angela Poorman

The path already exists for you. As you become willing, your yearning will increase. Yearning is like a signal fire announcing that you're ready for more. You don't have to look for the way, because the way exists inside you, within your chakras. When you indicate to the Universe that you are ready, "the way" will magically appear to you, as it has done for every soul since the beginning of time. Become willing. Become curious. Become ready. Do your internal healing work, then TRUST that your Infinite Creator has got you, and is leading you exactly where you're supposed to go.

Galactic Phases May Stimulate Evolution

George Van Tassel believes that it is the movement of our solar system through specific parts of the galaxy which invites spontaneous evolution of all species on earth. He says that we, as souls, and even planets, suns, and solar systems grow and evolve in distinct stages. Van Tassel teaches, "Each solar system (including each planet) must evolve through grades, even as babies learn to crawl before they can walk. ...As our solar system moves through space, its progression is into an ever-increasing frequency of vibration" (Van Tassel, 1999).

Van Tassel suggests that it is a function of our solar system's spiralized movement through the galaxy which opens doors for spontaneous evolution of every species on the planet. High frequency particles may trigger great "shifts of the ages" every time our solar system orbits this special part of the galaxy. As we move through special areas of space, clouds of charged photons signal the encoded information within our chakras to activate. Some people will choose to take advantage of this activation period, while others will choose to ignore it. The former will move forward into new densities, and the latter will most likely choose to remain where they are.

Have you noticed a large number of people becoming activated in the last five, ten or fifteen years? That's no accident.

We can see these drastic and sudden changes in the fossil records of Earth's history, written in the ancient rocks. Evolution doesn't happen at a slow and steady rate. Evolution is a relatively rapid change triggered by galactic phases. Remember, growth occurs in pulses.

What Will Others Experience When I Awaken?

Because Earth herself has not completely made the 4D shift, we're all still living in the same old bodies, walking around on the same old streets, under the same old sky. The Earth has not physically shifted yet, but many humans have made an opening. Something has changed about the newly heart-activated person. He's living in a 3D world, but he is different. He sees through new eyes. His heart has flowered open like a soft, tender bloom. He has brand new, powerful inner qualities. His self-perception as well as his perception of others is compassionate, easy, and accepting. His life circumstances may change completely. Old relationships may fall away while new ones come into being. He may feel a need to change his career, or move to a different city. He may feel called to do new work, focusing on completely different issues than before. He is new, but his friends and family may be their same old selves. They might notice that he is different. **He will KNOW he is.**

Some folks may appreciate his newfound ways, but those who are still asleep may resent him for changing. They may tell him he is wrong, or encourage him to go back to the way he was before. *The Law of One Series* tells us, "An adept is one which has freed himself, step after step, from the constraints of the thoughts, opinions, and bonds of other-selves. ...**[His] freedom is seen by [others] ...as evil**" (Elkins, 1984).

The Law of One is telling us that your unawakened friends will sense your "magical change," but will not likely understand what it means. Your friends' misunderstandings of what you have achieved may cause problems in your relationships. One of the most important tasks you must master when activating the heart chakra is to become compassionate for your enemies, as Jesus taught. You must free yourself from the judgments and opinions of others. You must accept and forgive yourself and your neighbor. (Yes, even when they hurt you or don't understand.)

There will come a day when humanity reaches critical mass. At that time, *Earth* will finally make her shift into Fourth Density. No one really knows what to expect. Earth changes, pandemics, governmental upheaval, financial crashes, and societal reorganization are prophesied.

One thing is certain — some humans will choose not to move on into Fourth Density. These people will stay in Third Density. There are many theories as to what these people will experience. Some say they will be moved to a new planet and "...the meek shall inherit the Earth." (Another way to express that statement is to say, "Pure-heartedness will become the way of the world.") Others believe that everyone will naturally die out, and the new generation of babies will be born fourth-density-activated, thus creating a homogenous 4D Earth. Whatever happens, the point is that the newly shifted 4Ders will live in a Fourth Density world, while people who choose to remain in 3D will be allowed to do so. The way it goes down is a mystery which we'll be finding out together as it unfolds.

At this time on planet Earth there are many people who have attained Fourth, Fifth, and even Sixth Density consciousness. They all live in regular human bodies, so no one can tell, upon first glance, who they are. The difference is on the level of their souls. A person can carry higher density consciousness within, while living in a Third Density world. Most of these folks are "Volunteer Souls" who have come to help Earth natives in their awakening. They are considered very wise. You may know a few. A couple of examples of evolved souls might be Martin Luther King, Jr. and Tony Robbins (who may have attained approximately 4D consciousness), Oprah Winfrey and Marianne Williamson (who may have attained approximately 5D consciousness), and Eckhart Tolle and Rumi (who may have attained approximately 6D consciousness). These souls have mastered high levels of love and wisdom, and have come to Earth to help during the Great Shift. I'll explain more about these **Volunteers** in chapter 13.

Ascension is not a new idea. Cultures from all over the world have been talking about the coming of The Great Shift throughout written history. All of them discuss going through some sort of great dissolution, which is simultaneously an *evolution* of the human being and the human body. William Henry calls the new body "the light body." He has compiled an incredible amount of information about the light body from many religions and spiritual texts from the world over.

Henry writes: "So, our goal is to create or perfect a light body? Yes, that is what every spiritual tradition says. And they all have a different name for it. In Sufism it is called **"the most sacred body"** and **"supra-celestial body."** Taoists call it **"the diamond body,"** and those who have attained it are called **"the immortals"** and **"the cloud-walkers."** Yogic schools and Tantrics call it **"the divine body."** In Kriya yoga it is called **"the body of bliss."** In Vedanta it is called **"the superconductive body."** In the alchemical tradition, the Emerald Tablet calls it **"the golden body."** The ancient Egyptians called it **"the luminous body or being."** This conception evolved into Gnosticism, where it is called **"the radiant body."** In the Hermetic Corpus (Egyptian writings), it is called **"the immortal body."** In the Mithraic liturgy it was called **"the perfect body."** In Christianity, it is called the **"Resurrection Body."** The philosopher Sri Aurobindo called it **"the divine body,"** and said it is composed of supramental substance" (Henry, 2016).

Whatever the name, all of these traditions are speaking about the same phenomenon: a being that has crossed over the vibrational gateway to the next dimension and has activated himself in body, mind, heart and soul.

Finding Your Spiritual Level

Hopefully, as you read through this book, you will be able to discern which level of consciousness your soul has remembered. I call it "your spiritual default setting." It is the density at which your soul is naturally vibrating. This spiritual station is your current leading edge of soul evolution.

According the The Law of One material, approximately 85 to 90 percent of humanity lives in the station of 3D at this time. My experience tells me that number isn't far off. As you read further, you'll gain vital clues as to whether or not you belong in the station of 3D with the majority, if you're a little ahead of the game, or if you are even a Volunteer Soul.

The most important job for each of us is to KNOW OURSELVES WELL, no matter which level we reside in. It is the entire purpose of Life.

How to Move Forward with This Book

The purpose of this book is to help you understand the system of soul evolution which has been in place in our universe since the beginning of time. Your soul evolves in a predictable way, just like your psychology develops in a predictable way. Every single soul who has come before you has traveled along the same Soul Map. Together, we will explore each level or station of awareness. In journeying through this book, keep your own thoughts, feelings and behaviors in mind. They will help you figure out your station. Be thinking about your friends and family, how they think, feel, and behave. You may become able to gauge the station of those people you know and love.

When you gain a general sense of the spiritual station of those around you, you'll better understand your relationships. Healthy communication occurs when you respond to your loved ones in ways that make sense to them, and in ways that will promote peace. Understanding other people's natures gives you insight into how to treat them.

If you are able to discern your spiritual station, you will finally understand your own behaviors, impulses, and drives. You'll also understand why you act like you do, and why you feel like you do. When you gain a sense of what's coming next in your soul's curriculum, you'll understand the meaning of your secret yearnings, desires, and bliss which lead you forward. You'll also become able to set realistic goals for yourself.

It is vital that you accept and validate the station you are in RIGHT NOW or you won't be able to use it for growth. Each spot in which you find yourself is a stepping stone to the next. Each stepping stone is essential. Learning to LOVE AND ACCEPT YOURSELF in each emotional state and soul density is the way to climb the ladder. Don't invalidate yourself by seeing your current station as unworthy. It is worthy! In fact, **you can't get to "there" without being "here."**

Please, please don't use this information to compare yourself to others. You are no better and no worse than anyone else. Everyone has a soul station. Everyone is growing and learning. The important thing is that YOU KNOW YOURSELF.

You may feel like you need to DO something to further yourself along your path. There is nothing to do but to subsist more often in the "being" than in the "doing." BE who you are right now, and BE okay with it! Feel what you feel right now, and BE ok with it! React however you react to your life at this moment, and accept yourself! **Your growth will take care of itself if you are present for it.** You are exactly where you're supposed to be at this moment in your eternal journey. There is no need to rush! Just keep plugging along. Strive to understand, and work to heal. Know that **the rose is perfect – whether it is still a bud, or it has blossomed into its fullest floral splendor!**

**You are a dazzling spark of Divinity,
gorgeous and perfectly-imperfect.**

The Path Has Already Been Paved for You

Many, many souls have gone before you in this evolutionary process. The Soul Map has been in place in our universe since the Big Bang. It's not possible for any human to think a thought which has never been thought before, because multitudes of generations of souls have gone before us, and all have experienced the same curriculum you are experiencing. They journeyed through Third Density on their way through the seven levels of creation, just the way you are now. **Your predecessors paved the way for you.** Energetic traces of their discoveries and insights can still be sensed because layered and encoded in the ethers of our realm.

Some say that these insights shared by those who have gone before us are housed within a place called the Akashic Records, a library of everything that has ever happened. The Akashic Records exist on an energetic frequency just outside our range of perception, but can be accessed by sensitives, psychics and adepts. Many scientists, writers, artists, and Creators claim to have dreamt the blueprints for their inventions, fully worked out. Many believe that these people have tapped into the Akashic Records (either purposefully or unintentionally) to access stored information.

Some people worry that they won't know how to walk their spiritual path. The truth is, every answer to every question is available both within and without you. All the information you need to evolve is encoded in your chakras. The answers are embedded in your questions. If you want to know what to do next, **ask within, listen closely, and watch your life**. Your life circumstances and your Emotional GPS System will show you what to do.

~ ~ ~

Now that we've set the ground work for how your soul learns and how it shifts to a new density, let's get into the good stuff! Let's take a close look at the path itself, the path upon which all souls travel on their way to reuniting with our beloved Creator.

~ SECTION TWO ~

A Trip through the Seven Levels of Reality

Chapter 5

The Birth of Your Soul

"...the whole nature of the Godhead
is to play that He is not."
~ Alan Watts

Why do I exist?

It is the question humans have asked themselves since the beginning of time.

Most ancient histories of Earth include a creation myth. When we read these stories through the *eyes of our hearts*, we begin to see that **all of the religions are attempting to teach us the same thing.** The following is my interpretation of all the ancient stories I have read, and what I understand behind the storylines of them all, when I read with the eye of my heart.

The Birth of Your Soul

In the beginning there was an omnipresent Source Field, an Intelligent Infinitude. This original state of consciousness was, and is, whole and unified. It knows everything and contains everything. In it, there is no time. All and nothing paradoxically coexist intertwined with one another. Within this eternal state of All-Knowing lives the potential for all that ever was, or ever will be.

As we continue to go deeper into the concepts behind the creation story, I will often call this omnipresent source, "God." Please feel free to insert any other name or gender you wish. I will be using the masculine pronoun for ease of reading, even though God is neither male nor female.

Since God knows everything, it is a *paradox* to say that He is missing some important things. But on a certain level, we can look at it that way.

What's the one thing that a perfect, omnipotent being can't do?

God Can't Experience LACK.

God, in His omnipotent state was incapable of experiencing deficiency of any kind. He was incapable of feeling the thrill of learning something He didn't already know (because God knows everything). He was incapable of discovering something new (because nothing is new to God). God wanted to experience a feeling he'd never felt before: *yearning*. **To feel yearning, one must first experience absence or lack.** God desired to create something from that yearning. These were things God had never done before.

So, God had a grand idea! He would create a *copy of Himself* (like a hologram), and the copy of Himself would be capable of having these exciting experiences. By experiencing life through his copied image, God would KNOW HIMSELF more completely.

In Sufism, it is said that God pulled a bit of light (a photon) from His face and looked at it. In doing so, He made Himself two. For the first time, God was able to see and love Himself in the second person. This separated bit of light was the very first creation. In Islam, this light/creation is called the "the Mohammadan Presence." In Christianity, it is called "the Christ Consciousness." Buddhists call this pure, unpolluted being, "the Buddha." Hinduism refers to the first created being as "Krishna." All of these are names for the same being, "The First Being of Light."

The Bible says that when God created the Earth, He said, "Let there be light." This was the moment when He pulled the photon from his face and created the First Being of Light. This

41

being of light is the "oversoul" of everyone and everything ever created.

The light from God's face was the first sentient being. The First Being of Light was the parent of all created entities, a perfect copy of his Creator. The First Being of Light knew everything God knew and was completely flawless. He was an exact reflection, a mirror image of God. God was flooded with love for the being He had made, and the First Being of Light returned God's love back to Him. **It was the very first reciprocal relationship.** How sweet and tender was this relationship! There was a moment of perfection between the heart of God and His Creation which reached beyond space and time, and still exists today. The First Being of Light was completely at peace; he felt safe and sound because he knew and understood everything. He knew he was Home.

The *first gift* which God bestowed upon the First Being was Free-Will. This gift was given by God to ensure that this Being would never become a puppet or a slave, but would possess his own free agency.

In order for God's plan to work, **He needed to bestow a *second gift*: a state of amnesia, or what I call the "Veil of Forgetfulness."**

Since the First Being of Light was one with God, he foresaw the plan which was soon to play out. The First Being of Light knew everything, and he completely agreed to the grand plan: he would submit to forgetting all he knew before. He SO LOVED GOD that he volunteered for the job. Even though he knew the risks in this new job, he consented without hesitation. It would be a gift of absolute love from child to Father, and it would be a gift of absolute love from Father to child.

At the snap of God's finger, the First Being of Light promptly fell into a deep sleep. He forgot everything he had ever known.

The meaning of "sleep" is forgetting.
The meaning of "awakening" is remembering.

The First Being of Light Lost his Memory

Suddenly, the First Being of Light became completely confused. He did not know who he was or what was happening. Here's the part in the story when our poor friend became frightened. He pondered the situation and saw that he *appeared* to be separate from his Source. Of course, he became terribly afraid and insecure. In forgetting that he was actually *everything*, the First Being of Light now believed he was only a small being, free-floating in an unknown reality. He suddenly saw himself as an imperfect, infinitesimal bit of the All. Our first friend felt shocked, small, alone, and totally terrified. He felt an abrupt, primal panic after being displaced from his home, his True Self who had not yet forgotten everything, and His Creator. Swirling in a fog of disorientation, he felt feelings of guilt and deep shame, believing that perhaps he had done something bad or wrong to cause God to ***abandon him.***

It is interesting to note, that when psychologists study children who have been hurt or abandoned by their parents, nearly all kids respond in the same manner. A child will believe that she *caused* her parent not to love her anymore because she *deserved to be punished.* Is this an ancient memory buried within each of us? Could those feelings of guilt and shame during the first moments after the birth of the First Being of Light, have trickled down to our human children, who commonly blame themselves for being abandoned?

These feelings of guilt and shame, found together with the feeling that one has done something wrong, are some of the most common emotions I encounter in my patients when they describe their feelings about God. They describe feeling unworthy of God's love. They reason, "Otherwise, why would He leave me all alone? Why would God allow bad things to happen in the world? Why would God ignore my prayers? Why would God let innocent children suffer?" The feelings of primal panic we have as human beings are reverberations of the original feelings we had so long ago, on the day we were created, on the day we were separated, at the moment we forgot the Truth.

It's important to understand that **the whole separation-abandonment thing was only a MISUNDERSTANDING.** You never did anything wrong. *God never abandoned you.* You and God agreed to this experiment together. Once you remember Who You Truly Are, and the process you're going through to return home, back to your Creator, you'll no longer feel unworthy or shameful before God. You'll feel relieved, deeply loved, and at peace. I'll walk you through all the stages to understanding your true purpose and destiny in the coming chapters.

The mistaken idea of separation from God and the panic that the First Being of Light experienced has been termed "Original Sin." It's an unfortunate term. Because of our misunderstanding, people tend to think of "sin" as something inherently bad. However...

Sin isn't proof that we're evil.
It's proof that we're confused.

To sin is to misunderstand. In this case, our friend misunderstood the situation. He had a mis-perception that he was separated from Source, when in reality he was never separated. It only seemed so *from his veiled state*. He forgot why God created him. God put His plan into place out of LOVE, not out of punishment, and not because of any sin. It wasn't rejection. It was a loving act that God "pulled the Light from His face."

In fact, God is so very merciful and compassionate that He feels everything His children feel. God feels every drop of his child's fear, confusion, shame, and guilt. He cried and still cries with His creation out of compassion. But there's something else we 3Ders don't understand. We don't understand that God is so completely BEYOND the entrapments of emotion that all He sees is the big picture. God knew that his created one was afraid, but that he was perfectly safe. He knew there was no real harm. Not even death is harmful in God's eyes. God only sees love, learning, growth and consciousness. So, while God knows all of our pain, and cries with us, He desires for us to WAKE UP out of the dream to see that none of that pain is real. It never was real.

What *is* real is that you are still in "Heaven," between the arms of your Creator, your Source, right now. The rest is all just a dream.

The Creation of the Multiverse

"The only thing the Creator ever made was one photon. Everything else fractalized off of that."
~ David Wilcock

On that day, God ignited a vibratory hum. The entirety of creation came into instantaneous being at just a single word: "Be." This was the sound of the vibration which sang out of the light, from God's face. It was the music of the soul. It is said that through the sound of that hum, a cascade effect has been put into motion that gave birth to all the worlds.

The Third Gift God Bestowed was the Ability to Create

**God created the First Being of Light,
and that Being created everything else.**

This is quite possibly the biggest misunderstanding among the people of Third Density at this time in history. We've been told that God created everything. But there's a problem with that. If God created everything, how can one explain all the pain and suffering humans endure? God, in His resplendent nature, would never, and *could* never create suffering for his own creation. God created The First Being of Light, and then The First Being of Light exploded with his own thoughts and beliefs. Some of his thoughts and feelings were coming from his true nature, as God's perfect reflection, and some were coming from his fear. His perfect thoughts, as well as his imperfect thoughts, created all the worlds. Yes – thoughts create reality.

How was this done? The entire created "multiverse" was generated by the **BELIEFS** of the First Being of Light. That is how powerful *your* beliefs are; they are powerful enough to create world upon world, realm upon realm. Since The First Being of Light was the original co-Creator, he created all the worlds through God's gift of free-will, or through his own consciousness. On the day of creation, each thought in the mind of the First Being of Light was so infused with GOD'S AUTHORITY, that it rapidly expressed outward. Both misperceptions and True-perceptions went forth and manifested themselves. The magnificent explosion of creation has been termed in scientific theory as the "Big Bang."

The "Big Bang" blasted forth so blindingly fast that all the cosmos was created in a matter of (what we would perceive as) seconds. All the stars, galaxies, planets, moons, people, animals, plants, atoms, quarks, dark matter - everything was created from the consciousness of the First Being of Light. It wasn't created directly by God. God left the creation of all the densities to His child.

From the mind of the First Being of Light cascaded forth all of the divisions. He is our forefather and our oversoul, like a tree which divides itself exponentially from trunk, to branches, to twigs, to leaves. The creation was divided into smaller and smaller seemingly separate pieces of the whole. Each new mirror image fractalized, eventually becoming innumerable individual souls - having individual consciousness themselves. *Each tiny bit still carries the perfect original essence of the Source.* Just like a hologram.

You are one of these divisions.

In reality, you are not separated from God, although *at your current level of evolution, it seems as though you are.*

The Creation of the Seven Level System

We can divide all of the cascading realities into seven major densities. The seven densities were generated from the top downward. The highest densities were created first. They hold the most light and remembrance of Original Essence. Clones of God's Majestic Qualities were replicated from one world down to succeeding realities. Holographic reflections tumbled into being. **Each became a less perfect "copy of a copy," down the line.** Each carried slightly less light than the last and became more distorted. Sixth Density was born out of Seventh, containing less light, and therefore less remembrance of the Truth. Fifth Density was born out of Sixth, containing less light, and less remembrance of the Truth. So on it went, all the way down the ladder to First Density, where the light is so dim, almost nothing of Original Truth is remembered. It's all God, the Truth has just been forgotten. Dark, still, and sleepy are the lower realms.

Darkness is not evil.
It is just a condition where beings are in
deep forgetfulness of God's Reality.

The created worlds, from the highest angelic world, all the way down to the bottom-most world, were each created in this manner: thought after thought, hologram after hologram, world after world, soul after soul. The upper four **Worlds of Light** contain more and clearer memory of Source. The lower three worlds contain less light and less memory of Source.

Fear breeds forgetfulness and shadow.

ALL of the densities that I'm about to describe are based on some level of distortion and forgetfulness. Yes — even the angelic realms have *slight* misperceptions of the Ultimate Truth. Even the Angels aren't perfect. How do we know? Because if they realized TOTAL Perfection for even one moment, they would instantaneously merge back home into Source. They would cease to exist as individual angels. If Earth were to suddenly and fully align with the Creator, it would unify back into Oneness as quick as a grease fire, and no material world would continue to exist as we know it.

The Qu'ran says, "If we had sent this Qur'an upon a mountain, you would see this mountain crumble and become weak from the fear of Allah," (Qur'an 59:21). What the Qu'ran is saying is if a mountain were exposed to Absolute Truth, it would disappear and no longer exist in the created world. **Upon exposure to the One Supreme Truth, any created thing will disappear from this world, and return to its True State of being in God's world of Light.** It will return to the world of the unseen Source.

In the Jewish Torah, Moses says to God, "Show me your glory." God told Moses that it would not be safe for any being to behold his splendor. God felt protective of Moses and instructed him, "Stand in the cleft of the rock... you will see My back, but My face must not be seen" (Exodus 33: 17-23).

When God reveals His Face to any created thing, it merges back into the Wholeness from where it originated.

To Conclude Our Story...

God wanted to experience each tiny bit of All That Is, and the plan was to do that vicariously through the eyes, ears, hands, and hearts of his beloved creations.

Even though Seventh Density was created first, *your soul begins its journey in First Density* — the sleepiest and darkest density. Why? Because the whole point is that **God yearns to experience lack and wants to experience waking up from it.** This is why we start at the most unaware density, and grow from there.

The truth is, you possess the ability to study tiny bits of creation with your perspective. As a human, you only see a tiny sliver of reality at a time. Your narrow viewpoint gives God the opportunity to narrow the aperture of His camera lens to focus on a pinpoint. Can you think of any holier job than to be the camera lens for God?

Some people feel that their inability to see the big picture, combined with a feeling of being here alone without information, are frustrating limitations in our lives. But these illusions are necessary. There was no choice for God but to limit our focus and give us amnesia. Why? Because otherwise, it would be impossible for an omnipotent being to experience a process of discovery when It already knows everything.

Remember, God has not abandoned you. As Muslims say, "He is closer to you than your jugular vein." It is your divine mission to learn for Him, to discover for Him, and to create for Him. Awakening is a process of remembering what you've forgotten. **Awakening is a process of remembering what you knew the moment of your "original birth," when God took the light from His face to create you as His reflection.**

Your job is to move from the most individuated, forgetful point of being, gradually back into the full awareness that All is One with the Source. How is this done? We accomplish it by undertaking a powerful, miraculous journey, as we make our way up through each density, guided by our inner Soul Map. We are making our way back home.

Chapter 6

The First Level of Soul Evolution

Unconscious Existence

God created the First Being of Light, then the First Being of Light created all the worlds through the process of fractalization, or divine geometry. The First Being of Light continued on to create billions of fragments which we think of as individuated, sentient souls. These souls are you, me, every plant, mineral, animal, every star, every planet, and every bit of intelligence that exists, everywhere. Each one, each *soul*, follows the same map back home. Each soul begins its journey in First Density.

First Density is the lowest world, where all beings are completely and totally asleep. After our rapid descent (which took only a split second), we found ourselves in First Density, freshly born from All That Is. In First Density, we were at our most unaware state. We had forgotten all of what we knew the moment we were born from the light of God's face.

First Density corresponds to the first chakra in the body, and the "red light ray" on the rainbow spectrum. The primary developmental milestone of this stage of growth is simply to **experience existence.**

Let's take a closer look at what your soul went through in the lowest created realm.

The First Level "Earth Kit"

When you arrived in the first soul level, you got your first "body" in a physical universe. There, you might have existed as an element on the periodic table, for example, an atom. As you evolved, you matured into rock, air, water, or fire. Your newly incarnated soul had forgotten everything. Your consciousness was that of a sleeping "being" without thought or self-awareness. Some believe essential elements like rocks aren't alive. But they're wrong. **There is an elemental consciousness at this level.** You once existed at this very basic, *sub-conscious* level of being!

A First Level Incarnation

Imagine that you lived as water in one of your First Density incarnations. We'll give you a name: Rainy. Good ole' H2O.

Rainy lived on earth in the form of a small stream. One day, a deer came up to Rainy for a drink. Rainy was intrigued in her watery way. Rainy experienced the deer very simply, but she did sense a sort of primitive acknowledgment of sentience. The deer drew her water gently into his mouth, and Rainy traveled down the deer's throat into his belly. Having this experience touched something very subtle within Rainy's primal intelligence. Water can't have a conscious thought. *But water does have a vibration, which is a low level of consciousness.* Interacting with beings who were more self-aware, like animals and people, helped Rainy to begin to recognize that she was also alive!

Remembering Who You Are in the First Level

Being around other primal elements and sentient beings helped to create an imprint within Rainy's soul. Her consciousness gathered all of these energy imprints, very slowly, over millennia… and Rainy learned. As she traveled through rivers and into oceans, as she evaporated into vapor and accumulated into the clouds, and finally, as she fell to the Earth as rain, she learned. Being absorbed by the soil and traveling deep into underground caverns and aquifers taught her about living as matter. Experiencing all of these different forms of herself helped her remember Who She Truly Is.

The same can be said for each First Density element. Throughout your tour in 1D, whether you lived a life as a crystal, a clump of dirt, a particle of mercury, an atom of oxygen, or a moon rock, you experienced all kinds of ways to exist as physical matter. And you learned.

Another First Level Incarnation

Imagine that in another lifetime in First Density, you were a highly evolved 1D being: a group of atoms which had formed as a crystalline structure. Your name was Krystal.

During Krystal's lifetime, even though she was highly evolved for First Density, a multi-atomic solid structure, she was still so fresh from source that she continued to be totally unconscious, although very innocent and pure. This is why people love nature so much. Spending time in nature helps humans slow down. It helps them to feel clean and purified.

Krystal radiated her soul essence in a pristine way. She was a unique "person," **the same soul she always had been and always would be**, only very much unaware of herself. Even though she was sleeping in a dream of amnesia, she loved it when a person picked her up and held her. Krystal had a rudimentary sense of being admired, and this ignited a slight remembrance, a recognition of something very faint, from her oldest flicker of memory with God. The experience of being held wasn't enough to jolt her into a conscious state, but she did experience the communion, and it did affect her awakening process.

First Density beings have a vibrational signature just like you do. They are not dead or lifeless, they are SOULS just like you and me, living through their very first stages of life. First Density elemental beings give people clues to their Divine Nature. They are inspiring! First Density beings aren't yet contaminated by emotions or thoughts. They are yet unencumbered by a survival instinct, by self-doubt, or feelings of shame or guilt. These elemental beings simply EXIST, and even though they don't know it, they POWER the whole created universe! It is from these core elements that the entirety of physical creation is possible. As elements on the periodic table are assembled in various ways, galaxies are built. Even human bodies are made of First Density elements and nothing more!

Every particle of existence is a spark of God. Every bit of matter is loved by our Creator. **Every being has an innate desire to wake up** through varying stages of awareness. They want to be re-united with their Source.

The draw of love FROM the Creator TO the Creator, encourages beings forward along the Soul Map.

As an elemental entity in First Density, once you experienced everything you could learn, you graduated to Second Density.

Chapter 7

The Second Level of Soul Evolution

Instinct

Second Density is the level where you had your first inkling of conscious awareness. Graduating from 1D to 2D meant you had a qualitative shift in your experience of what it feels like to be alive. In Second Density, you incarnated as plants and animals. Your developmental soul task was to develop a **conscious mastery of your physical form, your instincts, and your emotions**. Second Density corresponds to the second chakra in the body and the "orange light ray" of the visible spectrum.

In First Density, you existed but were not aware of yourself. In Second Density it was so much fun to **consciously experience yourself for the first time**. How exciting it was to evolve into a body that had the ability to feel physical sensation and emotion! As a late-stage Second Density animal, you even gained some rudimentary problem-solving skills. How utterly sensational that must have felt after spending eons of time as simple dirt or water!

Let's break things down even further. For the sake of imagination, let's say your soul spent a 2D lifetime incarnated as a dog. Your name was Sparky.

Your Second Density "Earth Kit"

When you incarnate into any density, you receive a special suit to wear. The Earth Kit is outfitted with the perfect instrumentation that you need to live, learn, and thrive within your current density. Your kit is comprised of three parts: a physical body, an emotional body, and a mental body. Each time you advance to a higher density, you'll get an upgraded kit. Your 2D Earth Kit is specialized precisely to help you make the most of Second Density and all there is to explore here.

In the early stages of this density you found yourself incarnating as lower plant life, like algae. You found it *thrilling* to experience yourself as algae because it was WAY more interesting than being a hydrogen atom!!! Souls learn enormous amounts of information at each stage of life (even the lower densities). When you were ready for more experience, you incarnated as flowering and fruiting plants, and finally trees. In the mid-to-late stages of Second Density, you spent many lifetimes incarnating as simple animals. Finally, you ended Second Density with a series of lives incarnating as more conscious animals like whales, dolphins, cats, dogs, and chimpanzees. The entire process of third level evolution takes many hundreds of thousands of years and countless incarnations. These higher-level 2D beings are becoming aware of their awareness.

A Second Level Incarnation

Sparky loved running fast. He loved his dinner. He got a lot of satisfaction out of socializing with other dogs, tumbling and roughhousing. Sparky was able to feel simple emotion. He felt sad when his master left the house, and he felt happy when she returned. He felt ashamed when he was scolded and proud when he did his "tricks!" Sparky even felt depressed when his animal and human friends went away or died.

Spirituality in the Second Soul Level

You, as Sparky, looked up to your master like she was a GOD. Why did you consider a human being to be your "God" when you lived as Sparky in Second Density? Because the human who took care of you held a higher level of consciousness than you did, and you sensed it. Sparky aspired to be like her.

Late-stage Second Density beings admire Third Density beings because they intuitively know that one day, they will evolve into 3D, too. Think about the way little kids feel around

61

big kids. They look up to them. They want to be like them. That's how late-stage Second Density beings feel about 3Ders. They're totally enamored.

In the late stages of Second Density when you were beginning to sense a glimmer of Third Density, more elementary rational thought began to emerge. This thinking wasn't yet as sophisticated as that of a human being, but you were getting close, and it was exhilarating!

Relationships with Others in the Second Soul Level

During your travels through Second Density, you were capable of forming relationships with other beings, but they were very simple. Sparky, the 2D dog, didn't think about how it would affect his master if he pooped on her carpet. He just did what his impulses told him to do. His humans may have wondered why Sparky could not easily be house trained. It may have been that the humans were expecting a dog to think like a human! Expecting a Second Density being to learn like a Third Density being will lead to frustration every time.

**A soul can think, learn, and behave
only at his own level of consciousness.**

Sparky is incapable of functioning any higher than 2D. Therefore, when we train a dog, we have to think like a Second Density being. This concept is going to be important as we study why people behave the way they do, so hang onto it.

Love in the Second Soul Level

Second Density beings, like plants and animals, can and do love. However, it's important to discern the difference between the ability to love at a Second Density level and the ability to love at a Third Density level. At each successive level, you achieve a qualitative expansion in the way you see yourself and the way you see others. You could say you see the universe through evolving "working models." You'll gain a new working model or understanding of the universe at each level of consciousness.

When you lived your lifetime as Sparky, as a high-level, Second Density incarnation, you experienced love with pure emotion, without any discernment about others' characters. You were capable of attachment. You simply became attached without thought, wisdom, or understanding of what love is. Dogs are undiscerning about whom they love. **A 2D dog can't deeply know his master, because he doesn't know HIMSELF yet.** You, as a Second Density being, *could* feel unconditional positive regard, and these feelings could be experienced as quite potent and meaningful emotions. Little did your second-density-self know what was to come. You thought, "This is pretty good as it is!" But it was about to get SO MUCH BETTER!

Society in the Second Soul Level

Second Density was the level where you began to learn about social structures. Who was "top dog?" What did it feel like to be accepted into the group - or rejected from it? What was it like to be hunted for food, or to be the hunter? You learned that you were stronger and safer as an accepted member of a tribe or a pack than you were on your own. In Second Density, souls learned how to protect themselves and their friends physically. It was all about "pack mentality." Sexual coupling was centered on satisfying the instinctive urge to procreate, and not much more.

Limitations and Struggles in the Second Soul Level

As incredible as all of this was, you, as Sparky, still had many limitations. For example, while you did possess a simple sense of yourself, it wasn't nearly as sophisticated as your master's sense of herself. As an animal, you could not self-reflect. You could not solve complex problems. You could not use verbal language.

These limitations are all *indicators we can use to diagnose* Second Density levels of consciousness. **When we observe a particular being's abilities and limitations it helps us determine the level of consciousness they have attained.**

Shifting to 3D

It's easy to see that learning builds upon itself. You in your lifetime as Sparky, were just about to bring all of the lessons you learned in 2D into the next level: the human experience. Your soul needed to experience all that 2D had to offer. Enlightenment cannot happen without going through each and every step. Each soul level offers essential developmental milestones upon which higher and more complex lessons are built.

As you began to awaken from the dream of Second Density, you started to **_yearn_** to be human. Yearning is the inner mechanism that draws you forward. You, as a human, may be able to see these behaviors in your household pets. Your dog or cat may almost seem like a human person to you. That's because they are very close to making their soul shift into Third Density. Can you imagine how marvelous that must be for them? Sure you can!

Have you heard of animals that have been trained to communicate with humans? Go online and look up "Bunny the dog." Alexis Devine is Bunny's human mom. Bunny's owner, Aleixis, has taught her to press buttons which sound out words. Astonishingly, Bunny is able to express complex ideas, more complex than anyone ever did expect from a 2D animal. She talks to her owner about her past, present and future, and she expresses feelings such as loneliness and love. The story about Bunny that is the most fascinating is when she punched out the words, "Who that?" She then walked over to the mirror, which her owner had placed on the floor. Bunny wanted to know if she was, indeed, seeing HER SELF in the mirror! This is extremely high-level thought. It is human-level thought. Bunny is a Second Density animal who is stepping through her gateway to Third Density RIGHT NOW – even as she still inhabits the body of a dog.

Another example is that of Coco the gorilla. Coco was taught sign language by her trainer, Dr. Francine "Penny" Patterson. There are many videos online of Coco signing to Penny with complex ideas. A fascinating moment was when Coco communicated to her trainers through sign language that she wanted a baby. They explained to her what needed to be done, and showed her pictures of male gorillas. In the end, Coco never found a mate that was up to her satisfaction, so they gave her a kitten instead. Coco named the kitten "Ball."

One time Coco ripped a sink out of a wall and blamed it on the kitten saying, "The cat did it." This is third-density-level, abstract thought. Language is a Third Density trait. Both Bunny and Coco are examples of very lucky ascending 2D animals that were fortunate enough to be given opportunities to express feelings and thoughts through words. Can you imagine how expansive that must feel for them? Sure you can! You were just like them at one time in your evolution.

I wonder how frustrated most transitioning animals must feel not to be able to express themselves in the way they want to?

Many humans feel the same frustration. Humans who are transitioning to higher stations do not yet have the upgraded brain or body to process or express all that they are beginning to experience within.

This is par for the course for the transitioning soul. As we sit on the cusp of the next density, we feel intense frustration, incredible longing and excitement! Some transitioning souls feel they're just marking time, waiting for the day they can start a new life in a new world.

Chapter 8

The Third Level of Soul Evolution

Service to Self

"The ego wants the same two things:
to pretend it is separate
and to pretend it is superior."

~ Richard Rohr

Third Density is the zone of the Soul Map where you become human. It is in this level of consciousness that you take on a body with an upgraded brain, and possess the ability for complex thought. This is the level where souls learn about who they are as individuals. Shifting from 2D to 3D means you will experience a qualitative change in understanding your own personality and the power of your will.

The primary developmental task of this level is **self-knowledge and self-empowerment.** It's a vital step because everyone has to realize who they are as an individual before they can move on to higher pursuits. **The lessons of ego have to come before the lessons of non-ego.** *There is no shame in that.* In 3D, you are learning about your personal self and what you can do. Third Density is the home of the lower, unpurified intellect. Third Density corresponds to the third chakra in the body and the "yellow ray" of the visible light spectrum.

When you graduated from a Second Density animal body to a Third Density human body, your animal nature remained, but a new component was added into the mix: an intellect. Animal nature combined with intellect is a tricky combination to manage. Here in the third level, you're still driven by your Second Density animal instincts, but you're smarter. Just like before, when you were in 2D, the impulse to attack your foes still now remains a powerful force within you. The big developmental difference is that you seldom do it with teeth and claws any longer, you now use opinion, judgment, and critique as weapons. It has often been said by mystics and seers that Third Density is the most difficult and painful spiritual terrain of all, because Third Density is a place where humans are learning to balance physical impulses with the logical self. The two make a difficult mixture to manage.

At this time in History,
Earth and most of her inhabitants
reside at the consciousness level of Third Density.

If you're a typical person living on planet Earth, your personal spiritual compass points firmly here, Third Density. As long as you're in a human body, you'll be dealing with your ego, but don't make that a negative thing. The ego is supposed to be in you, and you are supposed to get to know it.

This chapter is the longest one in the book. We've got a lot of information to discuss about where Earth currently stands on the Soul Map. We're going to spend plenty of time understanding our human psychology, our behaviors and impulses, and the real purposes behind them. When you understand the process, it will make your journey toward Unity with the Creator easier and a whole lot less confusing.

Remember – all the fine points we are getting ready to go over will help you determine your own spiritual station, and also help you to recognize the stations of other people. Is your soul at the level of 3D like the vast majority of human beings? Perhaps your soul has already achieved 4D consciousness. Let's find out by studying this soul level in detail.

The Experience of the Third Soul Level

You came into Third Density as a soul moving upward in consciousness. Despite the difficulty of this station, 3D is an exciting and extremely beautiful place. The material world itself is magnificent. The landscape, the mountains, streams, deserts, sunsets... all are just stunning. It is here that you get the pleasure and the honor of incarnating into an intricate human body and a newly upgraded brain. **You've earned an improved energy system in which your third chakra is activated for the very first time.** Third-chakra-activation gives you access to a whole new rank of self-awareness to explore!

Since souls, themselves, are genderless - neither male nor female - you may incarnate into a male or a female body at any given lifetime during your adventures in 3D. You'll probably incarnate tens of thousands, or even hundreds of thousands of times per density.

The third soul level is a busy place where you have many important lessons to master. You finally have the ability to think about what you think about... to introspect. You have taken on the ability to intellectualize and to philosophize. You have gained the ability to problem-solve with sophisticated mental acuity. You've developed the ability to project "if/then" hypotheses into the future, an important part of choice-making. Here in this level, you have evolved to the point where you are able to speak with verbal language and to write that language down. It occurs to you, for the first time, to tell stories of your past, and to document that history. You've become curious about science and how things work. You've developed a wonderful new ability to create. 3D humans have the capability to create music, machinery, art, medicine and buildings. You're also thinking abstractly, formulating theories and using your imagination to come up with unique ideas.

Third Density offers your first opportunity to begin working with the fundamental processes of manifestation; however, you're just beginning to get a glimpse of what conscious manifestation means at this point in your evolution. It won't really make sense yet because conscious manifestation is a 4D superpower, not a 3D ability.

PAIGE BARTHOLOMEW

Your Third Density "Earth Kit"

When you incarnate into any density, you receive a special suit to wear. The Earth Kit is outfitted with the perfect instrumentation that you need to live, learn, and thrive within your current density. Your kit is comprised of three parts: a physical body, an emotional body, and a mental body. Since you'll need specialized equipment for life in each density, the "suits" you'll incarnate into are unique for each level of evolution. Each time you advance to a higher density, you'll get an upgraded kit. Not only is the hardware more sophisticated, but the software and the applications are also more sophisticated. Your 3D Earth Kit is specialized precisely to help you make the most of Third Density and all there is to explore here.

Your Physical Body Kit

First things first. The Third Density body has to be dense. In fact, the whole world of 3D has to be dense. In order for you to master the developmental tasks of the third chakra, you need to be able to touch, smell, taste, hear, and see solid objects. **One of the most important lessons you're exploring at this stage is your ability to affect what's outside yourself.** In order to play with this concept from every angle, you need to be able to manipulate and investigate objects that are _not you_. Perceiving the *appearance* of separate people, animals, things, thoughts, and feelings is a vital conceptual milestone at this level. (You will eventually remember that nothing is separate, but for now, it is developmentally appropriate to believe things are distinct from each other.) We have to go through the experience of being a discrete individual before we can advance to higher experiences like Unity.

71

**The first step is to individuate.
Later, humans learn what it means to
reintegrate into Oneness.**

Your Emotional Body Kit

Your upgraded emotional body is closely connected to the physical limbic brain. The limbic brain is the seat of your emotions, and is located in the back of your head. It is sometimes referred to as the "reptilian brain." It operates in two ways: fear versus safety. In other words, Third Density emotion is still pretty primal. Your basic negative feelings at this stage of your evolution are anger, jealousy, and fear. Your basic positive emotions consist of artistic expression (mentally, emotionally and physically), feelings of satisfaction when you've achieved something you've worked hard for, and positive regard for others. We're still not mastering unconditional love yet. Here in 3D, we have to focus on developing all the other parts of ourselves first.

Back in Second Density, you used your **instincts** to survive. **In Third Density, you master the use of your personal will to meet your needs and wants.**

Your Mental Body Kit

Your new mental body expresses itself well, now that you've got your new state-of-the-art brain. Morality comes online as you begin to judge what is good or bad, right or wrong. You learn by experiencing positive and negative feedback. You learn by comparing and contrasting. **Reason has become the main mode by which information is processed** (as opposed to relying on instinct in 2D). 3Ders are very proud of their ability to use reason. Logic is the game of preference. It's fun to see what your mind can do! In 3D, you enjoy counting things. You enjoy collecting things. You judge your worth, and the worth of others, by comparing every difference you can imagine or perceive. Competition drives forward movement. You are interested in why things work the way they do. Incredible scientific discoveries are made as 3D humans inquire into the workings of the physical universe. Medical advancements speed forward. Technological innovations soar. People dive into literature and the expressive arts as they start to share stories with each other.

No matter what race, religion or region of the planet, humanity's mythological tales of light and dark have always pervaded its storylines. Joseph Campbell taught about the Power of Myth in his book by the same name. He told of the "Hero's Journey," which is the basic template for all human awakening (Campbell, 1988). Why? Because the Hero's Journey is the basic spiritual mission everyone undertakes in 3D. This is the mission that pulls you toward learning your greatest lessons in Third Density.

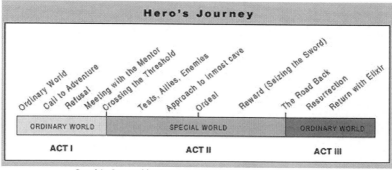

Graphic Created by Dan Brozite in his article,
The Hero's Journey - Mythic Structure of Joseph Campbell's Monomyth

73

We move through the same steps of the Hero's journey again and again, in small and profound ways all through our incarnations here in Third Density. Reliving this basic storyline expresses the curriculum which is hidden in your third chakra. The Hero's Journey is specific only to Third Density. We don't need it in later levels. The Hero's Journey helps you learn all about your individual self (3D self), and what you are supposed to achieve on behalf of God in this level.

Your Life will Show You What to Do

Within your body lies a set of driving directions, The Soul Map, to guide you on your travels through all the levels of evolution. There are seven major chakras which store all the information you need to navigate each soul level. Some religious traditions acknowledge the existence of many minor chakras which can be useful when studying certain aspects of human energetic design. However, for the purposes of examining soul evolution in this book, the Seven Chakra Model is the richest one for our purposes. The Universe shows us the number seven in many different ways. Prisms show us seven colors. Major religions refer to the seven levels of Heaven. There are seven notes in the chromatic musical scale. In the Bible, God created the world in seven days. The prophet Mohammad traveled through seven realms of reality during his Night Journey. Seven is the simplest way to breakdown the distinct levels of The Soul Map.

The third chakra corresponds to Third Density. It is located in the solar plexus, just below the xiphoid process at the diaphragm. Most people report feeling intense emotions in that spot within their bodies. Excitement, fear, attachment to another person, grief, and loss are all felt in the upper belly, the third chakra.

The entire learning curriculum required for Third Density is encoded in the third chakra. How does it guide you? **The third chakra provides you with inner desires and subconscious drives which will motivate you to complete your lessons.** Mostly unconscious, these yearnings and drives compel you to investigate, question, study, test, assess, and experiment with your outer environment, all the while learning who you are *in relation to it.* You can't fall off the path, and you can't get lost using The Soul Map. Whether you know it or not, you, and every soul, are constantly, yet unconsciously following your drives, yearnings, and deep inner desires. These impulses take you exactly where you are supposed to go! You don't have to be psychic, and you don't need a printed handbook in order to progress spiritually. **Simply following your best inner knowing** at every moment automatically brings you face to face with the lesson you need. **Your life will show you what to do next.** If a door closes, it means your chakra is guiding you to accept the roadblock and make a different choice. If things are working smoothly, it means you're going in the right direction! It's an infallible design. Trust your circumstances as a play-by-play guide for making the next, right move in life.

3D is not a realm of spiritual mastery. Later, as we move along our Soul Map we find that spiritual work becomes a deep personal commitment involving a desire to live by deeper truth. But for now, you're not very interested in those things. Right now, it's best to focus on the tasks that you ARE interested in. **Whatever you're interested in is what you're supposed to be paying attention to!** Curiosity is how we navigate our Soul Map.

The Ego in the Third Soul Level

The ego is at its strongest in 3D because it has a very important part to play in your evolution. The soul needs to learn all about itself, its own needs, and how to get those needs met. It uses the ego to get the work done. It's developmentally appropriate and necessary for you to put yourself first. **The ego is extremely polarized**, which unfortunately, causes people to judge one another and argue. Believe it or not, learning how to gain power over others is actually an important lesson. Although, of course, Third Density isn't the height of spiritual mastery, it is a necessary step on the road map. Just like a child has to learn addition and subtraction before he can understand multiplication and division, *you have to go through a selfish stage before you are capable of learning self-less-ness.*

Your ego will go to great lengths to make sure it comes out looking innocent, even at other people's expense. "The person who dies with the most toys wins" is a colloquialism that really does apply at this stage. Everybody believes that he is right and the other guy is wrong. Wars run rampant because everyone is fighting to get his way, but no one truly listens to the other. As barbaric as the ego may seem, it is actually an *improvement* over Second Density "instinct."

**The ego is the highest,
most sophisticated form of INSTINCT.**

The Ego's Thought System

Your ego has developed its own thought system. **The Ego tells you that you're a victim of your circumstances and that everything "out there" is to blame for your unhappiness.** The ego takes its limited thought system and believes it's real.

The ego's thought system is incomplete and incorrect. You don't yet have enough understanding about the true make-up of yourself, and so the ego makes up its own beliefs in an attempt to fill in the blanks. In a way, your ego is trying to help and protect you. (We'll get more into this concept when we discuss *Parts Work* in later sections.) Even though it may seem so, the ego isn't bad. It's a necessary tool for learning Who You Are. It's also great at helping you master the lessons of self-empowerment. I, for one, am grateful to mine for the way it tries to help me.

"Projection and blame" is a psychological strategy that your lower unpurified intellect has created to try to make sense out of the world. It's otherwise known as the "victim/perpetrator mentality." You'll either project all your negative feelings out onto others, or you'll attack yourself, projecting them within.

When you project your feelings outwardly, someone else gets to take the blame and hold your pain. When you project your feelings inwardly, you martyr yourself and take on the weight of the world. Either way, the ego always thinks it is SOMEONE'S FAULT! It's either theirs or yours.

All of this probably sounds pretty miserable. It IS a painful predicament. 3Ders don't completely understand spiritual Truth yet, but they're trying SO HARD to understand SOMETHING!

You'll be relieved to find out that it is NEITHER your fault - NOR their fault.

"Projection and blame" is not what God wants for his growing offspring. God is nothing but love. Because nothing but love is real, God wants only for you to remember what you were created for so you can free yourself from the ego's wretched

77

thought system. We truly don't see through the mist when we're living in Third Density, and we don't remember how to get happy and pain-free. Blaming is the ego's best attempt to make itself feel better. Unfortunately, it almost always fails.

We're confused. We're angry. We just want everything to be ok. We just want to feel comfortable. But we can never feel fully comfortable when we don't surrender our personalities to something higher. The personal 3D ego-self will promise us wealth, beauty, and youth. It will promise us vindication, revenge, and legitimacy. It will promise us pleasure, fame, and stature. It will promise us freedom. But of course, it can deliver none of these things.

All of this may sound like 3D is a savage spiritual station to go through, but when we look at the situation from a developmental perspective, these behaviors are normal and expected. This is the picture of our current world. **We are living in a Third Density, ego-driven world.** It's really not a bad thing developmentally-speaking. It's a giant leap forward from Second Density.

An Incarnation in the Third Level

Let's take a look at one of your own lifetimes in Third Density. In this incarnation you were freshly born, a beautiful, perfect baby boy. The midwife placed you into your mother's arms. "I will name you Adam," she cooed as she snuggled you into her breast and smelled your sweet hair.

Adam's parents loved him more than any human they had ever known. Unconditional love is difficult to come by in Third Density, and is felt most frequently by mothers and fathers toward their children, or between people and pets. (In the level of 3D consciousness, even romantic love is not yet fully unconditional.)

You, as Adam, had plenty to eat, a comfortable home, and a large family who cared for you very much. But there were imperfections, too. Dad drank too much and sometimes instigated loud, scary arguments with Momma. When Adam was three years old, another baby came. And then another. And another. There ended up being four children in all, living in a cramped home with unhappy parents at the helm. Was there enough love to go around? Sometimes it did not seem so. Often 3Ders experience feelings of lack. You as young Adam feared you were becoming invisible and unimportant.

School felt overwhelming, but there was no sympathy. "Making the grade" was something rigidly expected of kids whether one felt supported at school or not. Needless to say, you, as Adam, ended up feeling as if your difficulties did not matter to anyone. You were adrift, and felt frightened of school, of learning, and of authority figures.

As the years went by, you, as Adam, spent more and more time alone in the bedroom that you shared with your brother. The kids at school were sometimes mean, and the teachers were strict. Momma didn't have time to tend to many of Adam's deeper childhood needs for reassurance, affection, or cuddling, so Adam's bunkbed became his safe place. There, he could escape the pain and chaos of life. Because there wasn't enough support for Adam, stress began to pile up... **and IN**. These are common family stories which play themselves out in Third Density.

Children internalize the stressors in their families. Because they don't yet have fully developed brains, they believe that any difficulties happening in relationship with others are because THEY are somehow bad or wrong. Of course this is not the truth. Without the validation of a wise adult to explain the world to them, without a gentle, positive guide to *mirror a child back to himself*, kids tend to sink away into a fantasy world believing they are the cause of their family's unhappiness. It affects their self-esteem, sense of worthiness, and sense of lovability. Perhaps growing up as a human child is a reminder of that moment, long ago, when you separated from God and forgot the Truth. You felt alone and uninformed, without a parent to reassure you of WHO YOU ARE, and that all is well. That feeling of original terror will be repeated again and again throughout incarnations until you finally remember everything, integrate it, and make peace with it all.

We'll get back to Adam shortly. For now, let's discuss how social interaction typically looks in 3D.

Society in the Third Level

Socially speaking, you still need the herd to survive here in Third Density, just like you did in Second Density. However, an amazing revelation is dawning upon you. **You're realizing that you can affect your outer world through power over others**. This may seem negative, and in a sense it is. But from Creator's point of view, you must move through a selfish station in order to decide what kind of person you DON'T WANT to be. (Don't fall for spiritual advisors who tell you not to be selfish, angry, or to have your own opinion. Owning your feelings is healthy, but beware of using your emotions to cause harm to others.) Once you choose what kind of person you do want to be, you realize that others can contribute to your life, and you can contribute to theirs in positive ways. You begin to realize that friends and colleagues are invaluable when everyone works together as a team. It will be a deep and lengthy course of study to learn the ins and outs of *social negotiation* in Third Density. Give and take, compromise, offering, and receiving are important arenas to explore and practice throughout your lifetime. A big lesson is learning to share without letting your ego get in the way. This takes time and practice.

In high school, you, as Adam, reached a developmental stage where you felt a spontaneous desire to "look for yourself." Your Soul Map was firing up and speaking to you from the inside. Following your inner yearnings, you began to figure out how to be **accepted by the crowd** (a 3D lesson). You, as Adam, found the game of soccer, and with practice you got really good at it. In your sophomore year, you made the junior-varsity team. Girls started to notice you. The guys invited you to hang out after school. Finally, you had found a "place" for yourself in the world. The degree of **social status** (another 3D lesson) which soccer brought into your life made you feel very happy. You were learning so much about **working as a team with others, compromising, giving, and taking** (all 3D lessons). It was a chance to appreciate and respect others, while being appreciated and respected in return. All of these are important lessons 3Ders have to master.

Throughout your teen years, you, as Adam, were almost single-mindedly focused on friends and soccer. **It's normal for an adolescent to be completely focused on himself.** He needs to know himself fully before he can shift his focus outwardly to altruism.

In your incarnation as Adam, you experimented with marijuana and alcohol. All the kids were doing it. On one very unfortunate night, you were caught by the police, running away from a keg party. You were charged with "Minor in Possession" of alcohol. Your dad was so furious that he let you spend the night in juvenile detention jail – at the tender age of 16. "It will teach him a lesson," Dad fumed.

Unfortunately, the only "lesson" that you, as Adam, internalized was that Dad didn't care enough about you to be there. You carried that abandonment wound with you for the rest of your life. Again - here is another playing-out of original terror.

If experienced repeatedly, these sorts of betrayals by adults that kids so heavily rely upon for safety, would likely turn into what psychologists call "relational trauma." This type of trauma is caused by **improper attunement, inadequate attention, and the *absence* of acknowledgment for the pain** caretakers are causing the child. The trauma is worsened when there is no **attempt to repair the breech in trust.** These sorts of parenting mistakes happen all too frequently in Third Density. Many 3D parents simply don't have the spiritual maturity to love without hurting each other and their children. It's a very sad situation, and very hard to live through. But live through it Adam must, because it's a necessary stage in his soul's evolution.

The Experience of Love in the Third Level

Human love is very present in Third Density, but your soul's understanding of unconditional love is far from complete. **3D love is based on attachment, need, and desire.** Love in 3D is felt as intense positive regard. It may feel like true love, but it's nothing compared to the love you'll feel when your heart bursts open to Fourth Density consciousness. In 3D you are yet incapable of seeing others as they actually are; instead, you see them mostly as **projections of yourself.** When you strip off the shiny coverings, the truth is that a 3Der experiences love in terms of how the other person can serve his needs. It sounds harsh, but remember, 3D curriculum is all about learning to love yourself.

For instance, when children are full of energy, willful, or otherwise difficult for parents to manage, often a silent resentment or distance can begin to grow in the heart of the parent. Parents in 3D do love their children, but not perfectly or always unconditionally. Because 3Ders are still only capable of feeling an adolescent-soul-level of care for others, blockages to love can easily lead to neglect, abuse, misogyny, racism, unfaithfulness, divorce, and betrayal of all sorts (more 3D signature traits).

Because the 3D soul just hasn't achieved full knowledge of true empathy yet, relationships can be extremely difficult. Of course, as a soul advances into the late stages of Third Density, one's attitude toward love becomes more and more refined, but it still carries the same general self-serving undertones throughout the 3D experience. Remember the main agenda in Third Density? **It is to learn all about one's own power.** "What's good for me?" "What's bad for me?" "What do I like?" "What don't I like?" "What gratifies my fantasies, wishes, and wants, and what does not?"

"You get into pain because you turn Love into a business deal."

~ Sushant Sudhakaran

You, as a 3Der, are capable of caring for another. But the experience of true, pure compassion, the kind without a personal agenda, won't emerge until you cross over the boundary to Fourth Density where your heart chakra will become activated.

Still, learning about feelings is an incredibly pleasurable experience for your 3D-level soul. It's a huge leap of evolution to move from an incarnation as a Second Density animal to one as a Third Density human. Emotion is thick and complex here, and can be intoxicating! Emotion is an expression of Self. And who is your ultimate Self? God, of course. You are still the same Divine Being of Light that God drew from His face in the beginning. You've just forgotten it. Third Density love is a stepping stone on the Soul Map. Just one level of growth. Your inner Soul Map leads the way back home. You WILL eventually remember the big-picture Truth, step after step.

Adam's father had become colder and harsher over the years, and because you, in your incarnation as Adam were the oldest, your dad expected you to "set the perfect example" for your younger siblings. When you, as Adam didn't live up to your dad's expectations, **Dad withdrew his love** (a common 3D emotional reaction). It may have seemed like a reasonable way to help you, but by using *non-acceptance* as a teaching tool, he made a grave mistake which hurt your development and caused lifelong scars. We see it all too often in Third Density parenting. Often, Adam's dad hit him and yelled awful, damaging words to his son, words that eroded Adam's sense of worth.

In your lifetime as Adam, you finally became ready to learn how to **set boundaries** with your parents (a 3D lesson). Going away to college was a good first act of individuating from your family, as it offered you a chance to experience life away from your family's immediate influence.

Boundary-Making in the Third Level

Just as we expect a very young child to grab toys from other toddlers without any awareness of how the other children might feel about it, **the station of Third Density is where souls come to learn how to share on the cosmic playground.** We learn in stages and steps. We have to first realize that there *IS* a toy (1D consciousness). We then realize we *WANT* it, and as a result, we practice exerting our power to *TAKE* the toy (2D consciousness), and finally we learn to negotiate with other children to *SHARE* the toy (3D consciousness).

It's not just about reactively protecting yourself like an animal does in Second Density. It's more complex now. At this point, you're learning how to negotiate boundaries with others. Developmentally speaking – if bargaining for a toy cannot be done successfully, 3Ders will probably end up defaulting back to their 2D behavior of taking the toy by force. Until we learn how to bargain, we'll fall back into old ways. Even though 3D humans operate mostly out of self-centeredness, personal boundaries are still exercised in a more sophisticated way than they were in Second Density. You are learning and making progress!

Over the next several years, you, as Adam, floundered. Your grades were below average in University. You sought comfort through impersonal sex with strangers you met in bars, by drinking too much alcohol, and even sometimes by using cocaine and other dangerous drugs to numb your painful feelings and racing thoughts.

There were some good days, but Adam didn't really know what made him happy. He said to himself, "There must be more than this." He had no clue what that meant.

3Ders don't yet know what makes them feel relief, peace, or true joy. They tend to listen to the voice of their ego, because they have not yet learned how to listen to the true guidance of the heart. 3Ders are on a path of discovery. That's normal. It's your job to keep following your inner guidance until you, as Adam, can get closer to the "knowing" of 4D.

Girlfriends came and went. You, as Adam, became more and more disillusioned. You craved emotional intimacy and closeness, but didn't know how to get it – or keep it. Adam's life was feeling pretty directionless. You were a good-hearted young man. You wanted to do well, but your past haunted you. Your internalized feelings of unworthiness, created in childhood, tripped you up. The deep-seated relational trauma caused by inadequate care and attention in your childhood kept you twisted up inside – a spider web of internal chaos, pain, and negative thinking. You just couldn't find a smooth rhythm in your life. This is what is meant when sages speak about Third Density being the hardest density of all. It's filled with confusion, uncertainty, insecurity, and an overall clouded understanding of Who You Are and what all this is for.

Sex and Relationships in the Third Level

In Third Density, sex isn't only about satisfying the instinctive urge to procreate like it had been in Second Density. It's taken on an additional depth of meaning: an **opportunity to explore oneself.** Looking at it from the positive pole, sex involves playing with ideas of "Me" and "You" in a myriad of constellations. Mating rituals, competition, or roleplaying situations such as, "who is in charge," or "who is submissive," flirting, and coy games feel fun and tantalizing at the 3D stage of development. You're learning more about Who You Are through the coupling process.

Looking at it from the negative pole, intimate relationships in 3D are commonly laced with suspicion, jealousy, and possessiveness. Sex can also be used as a way to manipulate each other. It's sometimes used to gain financial security, to trick someone into marriage, to quell loneliness, or to boost one's self-esteem. All of these aspects are just part of the romantic picture at your level of evolution.

If you're identifying some 3D traits within yourself, don't feel badly. *We all go through 3D. Accept* where you are, *love* yourself for being perfectly imperfect, and set your sights on self-improvement.

Third Density sex is mainly focused on the self and so it intrinsically teaches us about our who we are. "How does this other person make <u>me</u> feel?" "Who do I think <u>I am</u> with him or her?" "Do <u>I</u> have power here?" "What strategies can I use to get

<u>my own</u> pleasure and emotional needs taken care of?" Sex in Third Density isn't too much about the other person's experience except for those rare peak experiences (which can be a wonderful taste of what's to come), or if you're incarnating in very late stages of Third Density.

At the age of 31, you as Adam, met Angie. Within five minutes of meeting, your whole world turned inside out. You fell into a fairytale-land of pastel dreams, a swirling translucent haze of Third Density love. Angie felt the same. Rushing hormones pulled them together with electro-magnetic forces beyond any human control. Strong subconscious childhood needs, long forgotten, came out to paint irresistible scenery in an impressionistic portrait of love. You and Angie came together like two puzzle pieces, fitting each other's projections with perfect accuracy. Angie saw nothing but flawlessness in Adam, and Adam saw nothing less than a perfect angel in Angie.

"Falling In Love" Has Everything to Do with Unconscious Wounds

There are dramatic forces at play behind Third Density love. *"Falling in love"* is more of a stage-play for mating and meeting unmet needs than for the expression of true, unconditional LOVE. **Your unhealed past informs the coupling process far more than most people realize.** When Third Density humans fall in love with one another it is impossible to separate their past from their present. Our sub-conscious minds know exactly what's going on. We sub-consciously spot the perfect match in a heartbeat.

But let us ask ourselves, "A perfect match for what?"

We attract our perfect match for working out our unconscious drives and emotional issues - our "blockages to love." It is totally up to us whether we choose to consciously address those blockages to love, or just ignore them. When we don't deal with them - relationships tend to break down. **Doing our inner work in 3D means working with our emotional wounds, especially in relationships.**

By now we can guess that the two decide to marry. You, as Adam, continue in your unfulfilling job, and do whatever you can to bring in money for the household. You manipulate people through your work, because you think that's what you have to do to get ahead. "Everyone does it," you reason. "Honesty doesn't make big money." (Again, common 3D ideas.)

By and by, Angie became pregnant. Deep in their unconscious souls, Angie and Adam had created the opportunity to have a baby in order to face many unhealed issues, and to learn more about unconditional love. These are exciting opportunities! You, as Adam, stepped up your hours at work so you and Angie could buy a little house in the city. It was idyllic. Safe streets, playgrounds and parks, a good school. It was a wonderful place to raise a family. Life could not have seemed better!

The couple truly wanted to believe it.

But, happiness is not easily held onto in Third Density. Why? **Because this is your soul's adolescent phase**. (Buying a house, getting a good job, the joy of a party with good friends, these are what 3Ders live for, but they don't realize they are temporary joys.) There are more unknowns than knowns yet. The inner Soul Map will continue to urge you forward – **usually through discomfort.** The inner guidance of the Soul Map urges us incessantly, "Look at your past wounds! Learn how to not to act them out in relationships! Learn how to heal! Don't stop here!

Don't get too comfortable at this level of learning. Keep moving forward!" It is our choice to listen to that inner guidance or not.

Adam and Angie's higher soul learning is really just beginning. In their early 30s, they are finally adult enough to begin processing their lives full-steam. (The brain's pre-frontal cortex doesn't fully complete its growth until around the age of 25. Biologically, you're not an adult until then, no matter how much society may support you to believe you are fully grown at the age of 18.) Together, and with a child on the way, the couple is, fortunately, stable enough to settle down. **It's in the process of settling down that gives a 3D human the opportunity to begin consciously facing his true inner work.** It's coming. Now the Soul Map fully kicks in.

Adam and Angie begin to sense a growing desire to search for more meaning in life. Their Soul Map sends out the signal, and the couple interprets it as a sign to seek more spirituality. They decide to find a church they like.

Religion and Spirituality in the Third Soul Level

Many Third Density souls feel that they need a mediator in order to talk to God. In 3D, to access God, you may believe you have to make some kind of formal plea; perhaps going inside a holy place to pray. You may go to Church, Synagogue, Mosque or Temple where it is thought that the leader maintains closer proximity to God and can speak on the parishioner's behalf. The overarching 3D belief is that the priest, pope, imam, or rabbi teaches the congregation about the secrets of God, and the congregation hopes God will have mercy upon them for being so sinful.

At each evolutionary position, religion manifests as a representation of one's level of consciousness. **God is always**

viewed as a manifestation of the highest version of oneself - for one cannot understand that which is beyond his own self. In 3D, God is seen as the "Great Rewarder and Punisher," because you have forgotten the Truth - you are not separate from God, and God doesn't punish Himself (therefore He doesn't punish you). In your current station, you see God as a separate entity that exists far away from you. God is viewed as the Judge of all that is right and wrong; the giver of both ease and hardship. From a 3D point of view, God is seen as someone who can grant requests – if you've been good enough! If you've not been good enough, you're likely to believe that God will punish you, give you difficulties, and maybe even stop loving you.

**Morality in 3D isn't based on a drive to be virtuous
but on an attempt
to avoid negative consequences.**

Remember, **sin is only a state of confusion**. The original definition of sin is to "miss the bull's eye." Sin isn't a moral judgment. It just means one didn't aim expertly enough. Sin is a mistaken idea which develops when we have forgotten the Truth. However, in your current level of understanding, you don't know that. Third Density religion has taught you that you're bad by virtue of your very existence. The world's religions have given you a strong message that an intermediary has to come in and save you from your wrongdoing, or else you'll burn in an everlasting lake of fire. You're taught that God is all good, and that humans are inherently unworthy. But how can that be, when humans are the pure expression of God Himself? You ARE God at the purest level of consciousness. 3Ders can't see any of this. They typically feel confused and conflicted over their worthiness.

The God that humans believe in is a projection of the Self. When a 3D being tries to conceptualize God, he imagines an unforgiving, selfish God, *because deep down, he is unforgiving and selfish.* In contrast, when a 4D being tries to conceptualize God, he imagines a loving God who cares for everyone equally and who uses love to create and heal all things, *because she, herself is all these things.* Why are the two views of God so different? Because a soul cannot see beyond what he or she currently knows. In each density, you can only conceptualize that which makes sense within your own spiritual rank.

Skepticism

We all know folks who are wary of things they cannot see, feel, or directly experience. Skepticism is a natural reaction to ideas which seem new or foreign. For instance, when a 3Der is confronted with ideas of angel visitations, crop circles, extra-sensory-perception, past lives, life after death, extra-terrestrials, or even the "touchy-feely" vibes of heart-centered humans, these things probably make him feel uncomfortable. Most 3D level humans believe such things are a bunch of "hooey."

Actually, the above occurrences are natural to Fourth Density worlds and above. It's just that the 3d veil keeps people unconscious.

3Ders often spend their time trying to *discredit* mystics and seers who speak of other-worldly events or even compassion-centered living. They rarely feel curiosity about such phenomena, they mainly they just feel judgment.

**It is fear of the unseen worlds
that creates an attitude of skepticism.**

Some people in Third Density choose not to believe in God. They may see the Universe as random, or as scientifically based, and not created by any Intelligence. Some 3Ders call themselves atheists or agnostics. But these are just names for a belief system that cannot see past its own fog of amnesia.

Money, Currency and Work in the Third Soul Level

Society, as Adam knows it, is captured in what some call the "Babylonian Money Magic" system, which is a weird-sounding term that describes a system of currency exchange at the heart of 3D trade. "Whoever can make the most money or get the most goodies, will enjoy the most comfort," goes the prevailing belief. He will have access to more resources, food, fuel, time, and luxury. Everyone else has to suffer with less. It's a lopsided way of living in a society where some people have more, while others have less. It has nothing to do with deservedness or basic human equality – and it is not based on need. It's a fascination with "me-power." Everyone tells you to shut your heart off and work, work, work. Some folks aren't built to shut up and work. They are the ones who suffer the most.

Money drives the world in Third Density. It's a damaging system that hurts everyone. It's also a way to keep humans enslaved by the almighty coin. We are controlled by our need to make enough money to survive. The system leaves little energy to pursue creative and spiritual ventures, and unfortunately, the elite want it that way. The ones in control are enjoying the system as they want it - **but not for much longer.** Things are beginning to change here on our planet Earth. A growing majority of humans are awakening to more and more truths. Love will prevail in the end, and Earth will be a very different place to live.

As humanity gets closer and closer to thinking with the heart, the exchange systems on the planet will change. Modifications may be very difficult to go through. But things will transform very soon. Things cannot stay as they are because our systems are unsustainable. Seeds of change are already sprouting. It's happened the same way for billions upon billions of years in our Universe – for countless planets and societies. Fourth Density will quite naturally bring fairness to commerce.

Perception of Time and Manifestation in the Third Soul Level

Third Density is one level of consciousness. **It came into being because of the sentience of The First Being of Light.** We then, made this place to give ourselves a world in which to learn 3D curriculum. You could say that this dense Third Density world *congealed*, or *manifested* into matter as a result of our collective consciousness. That's actually how all the densities come into being.

In this world of Third Density, time runs fairly slowly. There's an interval between what you wish for and receiving it – and that's called TIME. It is the waiting period between your thoughts and the manifestation of those thoughts. In other words, there is a time-lag between any plan and its fruition. Some thoughts have a very long lag-time, and others have shorter ones.

Adam and Angie have lots of dreams. "We want to buy a house." "We long to have a child." "We'd like to take a trip to France." "We'd love to make an extra $10,000." After any idea, fulfillment is never instant in Third Density. Time seems to run slowly in this world. Some people find the lag-time between an idea and its fruition frustrating. They want to create and manifest their desires more quickly! However, it cannot be so in Third Density.

The lag-time between making a decision and its appearance in your life is a blessing. You need time to think about, discern, and make sure of your choices before they manifest in your life. The time delay for manifestation is a built-in protection to save you from your undisciplined mind. Imagine what it would be like if every tiny thought each human had instantaneously expressed like magic? The world would be full of chaos and mayhem. Why? Because 3D souls are, for the most part focused on themselves - not on the good of the whole. For now, it's important that you focus on the learning what is in your own lap before attempting to become a master manifester. Your natural powers of instantaneous manifestation will begin to develop soon enough.

Besides, if you really think about it - would it be prudent for the Creator to hand over such instantaneous powers of manifestation superpowers to a soul who is still relatively limited in its development? Once you reach 4D and above, you'll naturally be ready and responsible enough to hold God's precious treasures for him.

While in 3D, you are still in the process of gleaning clues about the power which sleeps inside of you.

Science in the Third Soul Level

Newtonian physics is the highest form of scientific thinking that 3D can offer. Anything beyond it has either come by way of those special ones who've volunteered from higher worlds to bring new scientific ideas to the planet, or through our 3D scientists by way of a "peak state." During their peak states, 3D scientists experience rare insightful moments of opening to higher dimensional thought in order to receive ideas. Quantum physics is an example of fourth-density science leaking through to our 3D realm. The first quantum physicists cracked into the quantum world in the early 20th century via a peak state of higher density access. It was just about that time that we began to see the first glimmerings of Fourth Density thought streaming into humanity's consciousness.

We are so very close to shifting to Fourth Density. One signpost showing our proximity is that for the last 40 to 50 years we've been quite successful in developing Fourth Density medical technologies. Scientists and doctors have been able to "tune in" to Fourth Density consciousness to find a brand new understanding of the body, and have consistently discovered more astounding new treatments for health and healing.

The internet and technology of all sorts are blasting forward into 4D science. Think the shift hasn't begun? Think again. It has!

Never in the history of the world have we learned so much, so fast. The sheer volume and speed at which all this knowledge has been developed over the last 100 years or so **is a sign that we're nearing the maximum capacity that Third Density can offer**.

Third Density science, or Newtonian science, is pretty much maxed out. There is a limit, or a threshold, to the knowledge that can be achieved within each density, a glass ceiling, so to speak. When that threshold is reached, people start searching for the next breakthrough. These truly are breakthroughs, because what we humans are doing is **BREAKING**

THROUGH the barrier to the next density to find new insights, ideas and answers. We are at the tipping point!

A Word about Spiritual Arrogance

Spiritual teachers often talk about unity. They speak as though seeing oneself as "separate" is wrong. They sometimes teach in ways that make the lower mind (aka: the intellect) seem silly compared to higher ways of thought. Listening to some "spiritual people" talk can make us feel as though our Third Density stage of development is shamefully unevolved. **I DISAGREE.** Third Density isn't shameful. Third Density is a vital stage in our soul's development. Without all of the lessons we learn here, there's no way we could go forward. **Anyone who shames the concepts of Third Density is acting from his or her own ego.** A true higher being of Love would never discredit an essential step on a soul's journey.

Development of the ego is just one stair on the staircase. **We simply must solidify our personal self before we can take the next step upward.** The Sufis say, "Know yourself and you will know your Lord." At the 3D level, knowing yourself, and therefore knowing your Lord, rests on mastering your ego. The "Lord" created your ego for very good reasons. The ego isn't something to be embarrassed of or to try to get rid of. Our souls have to take one step at a time.

We have to solidify the concept of a SELF
before we can
understand the concept of NO-SELF.

Summing up the Third Soul Level

Third Density has got a harsh quality to it. That harsh feeling is a catalyst to push us to reach further. It works.... But it aches. You came into Third Density to develop your individuality. No one can move through many lifetimes in 3D without getting thoroughly hurt. Not just by others, but by yourself! Being a selfish a-hole hurts us from the inside out. Taking abuse from other selfish a-holes teaches us discernment, wisdom and strength, but the way of it sure does hurt. 3D is the school of hard knocks. It's the realm of tough love. It contains many enchantments, of course, but right alongside those pleasures come a deep sense of confusion, profound suffering and a stream of relentless challenges, one after the next. **It may seem cruel that we suffer in this way, but there is exquisite wisdom in the design.** The troubles of 3D propel us forward toward something far more soothing. If we had not experienced the pain and troubles, we might have sat in the shallow pleasures of this world, idling for eons, never feeling any *impulse to evolve*.

Third Density Earth contains a specifically focused lesson. Jesus figured it out, as did Gautama Buddha, Mohammad, Moses, Krishna, and many adepts and saints - both ancient and modern. **The focus of Third Density is to master both the beautiful power – and the dead-ends of personal identity.**

In the early stages of 3D, we arrived here feeling exuberant and ready to dive into all the exciting experiences that physical Third Density had to offer. We learned more about **Who We Are...**

- through relating to our friends, family, coworkers and strangers,
- by how we related to those whom we disliked, and those who we liked very much,
- by setting boundaries - and by getting them stomped on,
- when we were betrayed and when we betrayed others,
- when we were kind and when others were kind to us,

- through the struggle to survive, thrive and win,
- when we failed, when we succeeded, when we cooperated, and when we stepped on others to get what we wanted.
- by exploring microbes, atoms and stars,
- by studying the miraculous physical body,
- by studying the mystifying psyche and sub-conscious mind,
- by looking outward at our world - because even though we didn't know it yet - the world is a macrocosm of our inner selves.

In doing all of these things, we came into mastery of the core lessons of Third Density - **which is to know our personal power through and through.**

Nearing the End of Third Density

At some point in your 3D experience, the excitement of 3D began to wear off. It just wasn't satisfying anymore. You longed for more. **When this happened, it was your sign that you were nearing the end of your Third Density learning.** You sensed it was time to transform yourself. You, as Adam, were starting to question things. You were taking a second look at your life. The burden of the world had become heavy. Unfulfillment and restlessness replaced the wonder you felt when you first began incarnating into your 3D lifetimes. Adam found himself wanting something deeper. You, as Adam, sensed that you had a purpose just beyond reach, but you couldn't figure out what that purpose was. You felt lost. You did not know what was next. The Sufis say that the holiest of all states is "bewilderment." Why? Because it means you're about to make a huge leap in your spiritual development.

The feelings Adam was experiencing meant he had **hit the glass ceiling of Third Density and was just about ready to shift!**

Waking Up

When you begin to awaken from your Third Density dream, you'll start to see that those things which used to seem so awesome before are actually working against you. The judgments you assess against yourself and others are holding you back from the love, joy, and deep connection that you are longing for. **The competition that used to drive you to your highest highs is now keeping you from softening into the new consciousness you need.**

The Last Task of the Third Soul Level

Humanity is ready for the next step in its evolution NOW. Jesus and others knew that the next step in spiritual evolution meant moving into the level of the Heart. If you read Jesus' teachings, they are all about forgiveness and love. Jesus was an adept at the level of Fourth Density and above, so he was able to speak words that none had heard before at the time of his life on Earth. He was able to perform acts that none had seen before. It wasn't magic he was using to produce his miracles; he used a *function of his consciousness* to perform all of those Fourth Density deeds! We call them miracles. In reality they are powers which are natural to all the higher densities.

"Very truly I tell you, whoever believes in me will do the works I have been doing, and they will do even greater things than these, because I am going to the presence of my Father. "
~ Jesus; John 14:12

What Jesus meant when he said, "... whoever believes in me will do the works I have been doing, and they will do even greater things ..." was a message to humanity that they will soon be able to perform next-level superpowers. **Superpowers are what 3Ders call miracles.** What Jesus meant when he said

"...because I am going to the presence of my Father," was that he would soon be transitioning from Third Density into a higher density. This is something you, too, will be able to do.

The last action-step in Third Density to enter the 4D gateway is to **give up control.** This has to be total, so if you're going to meditate on one thing – let SURRENDER be the focus. You must give up trying to control your world through your will, as you know it. Your small ego-will thinks it knows how to manage things for you. Its entire goal is to maintain its rulership. It is misinformed. The ego puts you under its spell. The ego lies to you. You must continually let go of the ideas the ego feeds you. Surrender ego-feelings that motivate you in your life: like irritation, frustration, competing with others, vengeful feelings, needing to be right, protecting yourself from pain, wanting to be successful, rich, beautiful, skinny, buff, or special. All of these powerful motivators don't really work, but the ego keeps trying to use them anyway – because the ego wants *to stay in control of your spiritual path.*

Reject the ego's tricks.

Each day, meditate on **giving up control** of your relationships, the way your body feels, your finances, your thoughts and feelings.

When we reach the threshold of each new density, our last, and most vital task is always surrender. At each new density, there is a part of us that "leads the way." The ego leads in 3D. The heart leads in 4D. The soul leads in 5D. The spirit leads in 6D. At each level, the ego, heart, soul and spirit believe they know the right way. **They don't.** The fact is – we must take every tiny morsel of leadership away, and give the leadership back to the part of us that is in absolute union with God.

Allow yourself to admit that you do not understand. Let your mind become like that of a child. Let your mind become empty and ready to be filled with something completely new and wonderful. **Open your heart and ASK Love to present itself to you in a way you never felt before.**

Switching from listening to the <u>urgings of the ego</u> to listening to the <u>yearnings of the heart</u> is the way to let go of the ego's control. You might measure your progress on your spiritual path by noticing how much time you spend listening to the thoughts of your heart, versus listening to the thoughts of your ego. (Stinkin' thinkin'.)

The entrance to Fourth Density is a vibrational gateway. Your spirit must become the frequency of the gateway. Practice letting go of your ego's control. Surrendering control is the way to enter 4D.

**The last task of Third Density is to
LET ALL OF YOUR LIMITED EGO BELIEFS GO.
They are false anyway,
and they don't work.**

Accept Yourself and Be Nice to Yourself

As you are ascending up the scale of Third Density, remember to be very kind to yourself. You are not wrong in how you're accomplishing your purpose. You are perfect in the eyes of God and the beings of higher love. You are doing exactly what you are developmentally programmed to do. **You are not supposed to remember everything right now.** Open your heart more, trust that you are where you're supposed to be, and more will be shown to you.

Chapter 9

The Fourth Level of Soul Evolution

Service to All, Equally

"Compassion is a state of being
that helps us all remember that we are not separate,
that we are all in this great game of life together,
and that going about it alone is not effective or rewarding."
~ The Power Path, by Jose Stevens

Our Earth is in the process of shifting into Fourth Density now. Earth is already beginning to vibrate at a 4D consciousness, although it still occupies a 3D physical form. The folks who are standing by to shift have one foot in each world, so to speak. Because Fourth Density is energetically available, those who are ready are beginning to live 4D principles NOW. We've been slowly transforming for at least 40 years. It is a very special time – an event that mystics, sages and seers have been waiting on for eons.

For the time being, *those individuals who are ready for Fourth Density are permitted to cross over into Fourth Density mentally, emotionally and spiritually, but not yet physically.* When Earth is ready, all of the graduating humans will experience an incredible change in their physical bodies along with the planet they live on. Just like a caterpillar emerging from a chrysalis, humans will find themselves emerging into a whole new life along with their beloved sphere.

When you're ready to shift into Fourth Density, you will feel a dramatic change in your ideas and in your heart. You'll know when you're ready because Third Density concepts will begin to feel drearily outmoded and immature, or even *completely intolerable*. This is a natural feeling, one that is necessary to make the shift. Fear not! The repulsive feeling will fade and all will integrate in time.

When you graduate from Third Density to Fourth Density, your elemental nature (1D), animal nature (2D), and intellectual nature (3D) will remain, but they will **transform into a purified state of the heart**. Your lower natures will FINALLY no longer be in control. In addition to everything you've learned before, a new component will be added into the mix: **unconditional compassion.**

When you were in Third Density, you may have felt a type of compassion. You probably even experienced many "peak states" of unconditional love. But in 4D, compassion will fully open the flower of your heart. Once you've crossed over into the 4D level of consciousness, you'll *see for sure* that you weren't able to use love to its fullest degree. The difference in 4D is striking because the joy that comes from the magic of love has a totally different vibration. You just didn't notice it then.

In 3D, you were invested in exerting your own will. You did this through selfish means and various forms of self-centered boundary setting. In 4D, you'll have a change of vision. You'll realize that other's needs are as important as your own. You'll have a deep desire to make sure everyone gets what they want and need (not just yourself). There will be no more fighting. Peace will prevail on Earth – finally.

Encoded in your fourth chakra are the tools you need to learn about the following attributes:

- Learning to live in total sincerity,
- Learning the similarity between kindness and boundaries. Are they really two opposite things?
- Living in a virtuous way,
- What does "True Morality" mean?
- Heartfulness, Intuition, Empathy,
- Being with relationships in a new way, where deep Interest in other's experiences elicits your unexpected joy,
- Becoming aware of what *you* need and want, and learning to share your needs and wants with another.

The Experience of the Fourth Soul Level

Shifting from 3D to 4D means moving out of your ego and making a qualitative change in your understanding about love. Shifting from a mindset where logic was your primary mode of interpreting information, to a place where intuition is your primary sensing tool. Intuition is sometimes illogical, so this will be a big change and may take some time to get used to. **You'll stop focusing so much on *content,* and realize that *context carries more information*.** You'll see things less objectively and more subjectively.

The primary developmental task throughout your incarnations in 4D will be **to master compassion for yourself and others equally.**

How is this done? **Through radical acceptance.** No cheating or half-assing it. Mastering compassion means total, wholly comprehensive acceptance.

Fourth Density corresponds to the fourth chakra in the body and the "green light ray" on the visible spectrum. This spiritual station marks the center point on your journey through the densities. Physically, the fourth chakra lies directly in between the lower three chakras and the upper three chakras. Cosmologically, Fourth Density is sandwiched directly between the lower three "physical" realms, and the upper three "spiritual" realms. Fourth Density is the balancing point between "above and below." The lower and upper realms of consciousness are fundamentally different from one another, so the heart plays an important role. The heart is the translator between lower and upper realms.

ACCEPTANCE connects us to each other safely.
LOVE translates and communicates information.
Acceptance and Love are very close in vibration.

Your Fourth Density Kit

When you incarnate into any density, you will receive a body/mind or a special suit to wear, which will outfit you with everything you need to get along in that realm. Each time you advance to a higher density, you'll get an upgraded kit. Not only is the hardware more sophisticated, but so are the software and the applications. The 4D Kit consists of a physical body, a mental body, and an emotional body.

Your Physical Kit

Earth hasn't shifted to physical Fourth Density material yet. When it does, her body will change, and so will yours. Once the change happens, 4D Earth will still hold a type of material form, but it will be much more etheric and less dense. Because your own body will be like the Earth's, it will be composed of a much higher degree of light. You'll need to learn how to care for it in a whole new way. Food, sounds, lights, fragrances, touch, inert radiation, radio waves, astronomy and other etheric stimuli might overwhelm you. It may feel quite strange compared to the robust Third Density physicality you recently gave up.

You may already be feeling sensations such as these. If so, you've likely already shifted into the emotional, mental and energetic templates of the Fourth Density world, although not yet 4D physical.

Fourth Density IS NOT A WORLD OF LIGHT. Fourth Density is physical, similar to the Third Density world. Once you've shifted over to 4D, your body will contain much more light than matter, but it will still have a material structure. Fourth Density is the "intermediary realm" in between physicality and energy. Not until you get to Fifth Density will your body transform fully into light. In

107

5D, solid matter will no longer be possible, as everything will begin to vibrate beyond the speed of light.

Your Mental Kit

Back in 3D, comparing and contrasting, judging and competing were how you learned. But you won't need to do it that way anymore. Since the art of reason was mastered in 3D, you'll be into using a much more subtle and stabilized form of perception. The heart can think. According to The Institute of HeartMath, science is showing us that the heart has a small brain within it (Childre, 1991). Did you know that your heart contains a cluster of 40,000 neurons? We'll use the brain cells in our heart to think about, intuit and sense our world.

The process of thinking in 4D is achieved by a combination of primal existence (1D), instinct (2D), intellect (3D) and empathic perception (4D). Utilized together, we learn to *"feel into"* to gain information.

As your heart opens to receive information in new ways, you'll be inclined toward inclusion instead of the exclusionary focus of Third Density. You'll find you love discovering similarities among people, while accepting and appreciating their differences too. It feels so much warmer and happier!

"Our task must be to free ourselves
by widening our circle of compassion
to embrace all living creatures
and the whole of nature and its beauty."
~ Albert Einstein

Your Emotional Kit

For contrast, let's take a look back at 3D, when the emotional body was closely connected to the limbic brain and still pretty primal. **Negative emotions like anger, jealousy, and fear swelled in the solar plexus whenever you got upset.**

The central *positive emotion* in 3D consisted mostly of the satisfaction you felt when you achieved something you wanted.

When you shift into Fourth Density, all of that will seem selfish and childish. You will have grown to a point where Unconditional Love leads. In 4D, pain feels much different because the lower chakras have been mostly purified. Negative emotion is felt through the heart instead of the lower chakras or the animal brain. You will still get hurt, but the emotions will feel more refined, and less violent than before. **The 4D heart experiences NEGATIVE EMOTION in subtler ways, such as feelings of being mis-attuned to, not mattering, not believed, unheard, or feeling misunderstood.**

Your main POSITIVE EMOTION in 4D is the feeling of fulfilment when everyone's needs are met and all is harmonious. In fact – you won't feel satisfied until *everyone* is OK.

The work that you must do throughout 4D is your "gut work." Leftover residual feelings that still reside in the lower chakras may need to be cleared. In 4D, you'll be working to purify those old leftover emotions. In many ways, you weren't ready to fully do this work until now. You must sift through every aspect of lower emotion until you break through all the veils.

Emotions are important because they teach you who you are in the lower three levels, but ultimately - lower emotions must be transcended and let go. The heart level, or the Fourth Density, is where emotions are surrendered. This doesn't mean you should try to erase your emotions. It doesn't mean you should try to stop them or block them. It means you must work all the way through your feelings, using your heart as a transformer until you come to realize *the secret* at the end. The secret is this: **all emotions are reactive symptoms which SHOW US WHERE there are *blocks to Love*.**

Finding your blocks to love is the first step. The second step is to transform blocks through a process of acceptance, understanding and forgiving. When you possess Fourth Density consciousness, you'll practice healing and letting go of emotions which are too small to fit you anymore. Eventually, your emotions won't rule you any longer. They'll no longer have the power to hijack you. **That is what the Master of the heart chakra looks like.**

An Incarnation in the Fourth Soul Level

Meet Aurora. She's you, living a 4D lifetime. Aurora was born into a very different world than Adam. Aurora is a human, but a far more advanced one. She was born from a mother and father, she (probably) lives on a 4D planet, has a home, a family and many loved ones. She is lighter in body, but still physical. There is a feeling of spaciousness in her body because the density of 3D has dispersed and has given over to a much more sensitive and delicate physical presence. Her entire system is wired differently than before – because she's got a "4D Kit" now.

You, as Aurora, now realize how limited you were in Third Density. It feels like a whole different universe! In order for you to have made the shift from 3D to 4D, you had to fully accept yourself and everyone else – the good and the bad. It was necessary to accept both the narrow thinking and the expansive thinking. All parts have a right to be accepted as OK. It was sometimes gut-wrenching work, but worth it. Once you were past all of that personal purification work, it felt like unpolluted relief and freedom. Life is so much easier and more pleasant in Fourth Density.

Your New Heart-Skills

Before, in 3D, **you were invested in learning how to get all of your needs met using your personal will**. It was your main developmental task. You were able to see others' needs by observing their distress, and *sympathizing* with their situations.

In 4D, you'll suddenly have a profound change of insight. Instead of seeing people as separate others and guessing what they might be feeling and thinking, you'll be able to use your heart to *feel into another's experience.* "Oh my dear brother, I feel your deep agony and grief as if it were my own. I get you." **It's an evolutionary leap from sympathy to EMPATHY.**

You'll no longer have to assume what others go through, because *you will be able to sense what they go through.* Shifting into Fourth Density literally means adding a sixth sense. **It is the ability to know things by filtering them through the heart** (otherwise known as intuition). Can you do this already? If so, you are in some part fourth chakra activated.

Empathy, knowing, understanding, and acceptance are all synonymous with LOVING.

When you're able to accept someone you HAVE FIRST COME to UNDERSTAND, it is a complete action. It's KNOWING THEM through and through (the good, the bad and ugly), and then choosing to be ok with who they are.

Trying to accept someone you don't really "get" is like agreeing to disagree - which is a 3D phenomenon. Compromise is not a function of unconditional love.

All of these heart-skills put together lead to **forgiveness** (or integration of conflict). Living in Fourth Density is the first time you'll be able to understand what true empathy, understanding, acceptance and loving mean.

"True understanding is not native to third chakra.
It only comes into focus with Fourth Density activation."
~ Scott Mandelker

The Spiritual Aspect of the Fourth Soul Level

The spiritual heart is also sometimes called the heart chakra or the green ray because it is the 4th level of spiritual evolution for us souls. Your fourth chakra is strengthened by practicing love. How does one practice love? We practice love by walking a mile in another person's shoes, so that we understand what it's like to be them. We practice love by extending compassion for others, accepting and overlooking their weaknesses and forgiving their shortcomings. We practice love by being gentle with ourselves through the process.

We practice love by remembering our divine nature and by living in our divine nature as often as we can. We practice love by remembering our Creator and giving and receiving love to and from Him/Her. We practice love by being mindful of our thoughts, our speech and our actions. We practice love by being scrupulously honest with ourselves and with others. We practice love by keeping our commitments to each other. We practice love by honoring and allowing the free-will of others. We practice love by asking ourselves if we are thinking, speaking and behaving with a soft heart. We practice love in little steps every day.

We're not perfect - we're human. We are "perfectly imperfect." You, as Aurora, know you are not perfect. You are only halfway up the ladder to achieving perfect oneness with All-That-Is. But that doesn't bother you. You know that it's ok to be exactly where you are. You ACCEPT yourself and your life, because it feels pleasant to learn through love. It's a gentle process of unfoldment.

The Social Aspect of the Fourth Soul Level

Before, when you lived multiple lifetimes throughout Third Density, you may not have wanted to hurt others, but if that's what it took to make sure your own desires were met — sometimes you did what you had to do. In 4D, you, as Aurora, realize that when you step on someone else, it injures YOU. You, as Aurora, realize that you can't tolerate the idea of starving children anymore. The idea of poverty really bothers you. The thought that some people might have so much while others might have so little keeps you awake at night. Your heart has opened to the point where you can't go back to the selfish ways of your past. **Justice is a natural function of empathy.**

Social relationships will revolve around the idea of cooperation. There's an innate knowing at the Fourth Density level: **everyone can have their basic needs met, and no one has to go without**. There is enough for everyone. Using the 3D logical mind to figure out solutions to problems like hunger and poverty was awkward and ineffective. But the heart knows what the unpurified intellect will never know. The 4D heart finds new solutions to inequality that no 3Der was capable of finding.

You can see that many people on Earth today are thinking in this heart-centered fashion already. They are the change-agents of our time. Brilliant scientists, sociologists and teachers are the visionaries. Grassroots groups are everywhere. These people are awakening into the consciousness of Fourth Density. Yes. Right here, right now. You may be one of them!

"Fourth Density is feeling the understanding with your heart."

~ Kacey Samiee

Balancing Love for Self, with Love for Other

You, as Aurora, have come a long way since your days playing with arrogance and self-centered egotism back in 3D. However, you now find yourself in a different predicament. You are so aware of not wanting to be selfish anymore that you sometimes swing too far in the other direction. You struggle with how to give equally to yourself and to others. Sometimes, you put what other people want above your own needs. Sometimes, you go along with what the group needs at your own expense. You occasionally say yes when you really want to say no because you think it's the *"more loving thing to do,"* You, as Aurora, are still trying to find balance between loving yourself and loving others.

Boundaries take on a new meaning in Fourth Density. Healthy boundaries are important because they help us protect ourselves. There's a difference between a 3D boundary, and a 4D boundary. A 3D boundary would keep another person, whom you may deem as toxic, at a distance from yourself. 3D pushes away. It is the "negative" direction of self-care. Boundaries can go in a "positive" direction too: this would be the new 4D way. In Fourth Density, to keep a boundary you may want to imagine a love-

114

bubble around you that keeps your energy-vibration high. Inside that love bubble, you will want to keep your thoughts clean. You'll want to be nice to yourself. You'll want to keep your inner system well-regulated. 3D boundaries are aggressive and keep people out. 4D self-care boundaries are love-oriented and are ultimately good for everyone. 4D boundaries mean you're the "keeper of the vibration" – both for yourself, and also for others. Your self-care reverberates out to affect everyone. Softness is the new self-protector.

Finding perfect balance, loving others, self, and all things equally is the big developmental task of 4D. It will take Aurora some time and practice in order to really nail this lesson, but that's what Fourth Density incarnations are for. She'll learn that negotiating the thoughts, wants and needs of all parties is the ONLY way for a society to truly love its way into harmonious solutions. **She will eventually realize that it is NOT selfish to speak her mind and state her needs. In fact – it is a service to the group to do so.**

Learning the lesson of balanced love can be a painful process. When she believes she's not loving others properly, it can make Aurora feel bad about herself and confused about what's right.

Sex and Relationships in the Fourth Soul Level

It's important to know that in each density intimate relationships show up profoundly differently. In 2D, sexual coupling was all about meeting one's instinctive drives. In 3D, you explored all the ways you could learn about *yourself* by projecting your inner schemas onto your partner. In 4D, there is a deep interest in knowing one's partner – who they really are, what makes them a unique human. 4D romantic love is all about accepting the reality of a person, sharing, and kind-heartedness.

You are exploring your ability to love yourself fully <u>AND</u> to love another fully. This brings a whole new richness, connection, and intimacy to sex that could not have been understood before. Relationships are far less contentious. Outdated behaviors like clamoring to get attention or to have your attachment needs met are much less emotionally charged. You are learning to meet your own needs within, so the old push-pull dynamic in attachment negotiations rapidly fades. Relationships are based on safety, calmness and fairness. **Remember – the 4D heart is extremely concerned that everyone feels complete, and that everyone has gotten what they need.**

In your incarnation as Aurora, you meet a man and fall deeply in love with him. You notice that falling in love feels different than before. It doesn't carry the same intensity of lust, or of wanting the guy to be perfect, hot, or successful. This feels more like a soul-bond. Aurora and Carwyn look into each other's hearts – not just at each other's bodies. Yes, there is a physical feeling of sensuality between them. The difference is that it's balanced by unconditional love that creates an abiding delight and commitment in each other. Therefore, 4D romantic love is deeper, far more refined and longer-lasting than 3D sexual fascination.

You notice that you don't need Carwyn to be any certain thing to meet your expectations, and he doesn't need you to be a certain way either. You both simply enjoy each other. You both respect and honor each other's similarities and differences. What a concept! Loving someone without the need to work out hidden childhood wounds with a partner actually feels pretty free! It makes room for joy, curiosity and play!

You, as Aurora, and your beau Carwyn spend time learning how each other's emotional make-up. It's important to each of you to communicate in a way that doesn't contain violence of any sort. Relating is based on true respect for each other's needs and desires. Carwyn simply wants to discover and adore Aurora. And Aurora loves whom she sees in Carwyn.

It's important to note that sexual diversity begins to emerge rapidly in Fourth Density. People identifying as lesbian, gay, bisexual, transgender, gender fluid, bi-gender, intersex, asexual, questioning, etc., suddenly becomes very common. Why? **Because humans are beginning to look into the SOULS of their partners, not as they did in Third Density when they often looked at their partners' bodies or genders.** Love shows up everywhere, in all ways, in all forms, in all bodies. Romantically speaking, the Fourth Density heart just wants to share love without so many ego limitations.

Science in the Fourth Soul Level

It's an exciting time for science of all kinds. Humanity will cross the bridge between the old-model of Newtonian physics, into the new *Science of Consciousness.* The science of conscious is what we call Quantum physics.

Quantum physics has proven that the presence of an observer affects the behavior of that which is observed. This fact alone raises paradigm-shattering questions about the nature of reality. It suggests that the observed and the observer are linked. Perhaps they are in some kind of mystifying, personal communication. Maybe they are even the SAME BEING. Here in 4D you'll learn that materiality is, in fact, an illusion. Your view of the world which seemed so real to you ever since your entry into First Density will change completely. When you reach Fourth Density you'll begin to see just how pliable and plastic the physical planes really are.

There's a very interesting concept in quantum theory called "entanglement." It means that two or more particles do not behave like separate objects, as we might expect. In an article entitled, *How Quantum Entanglement Works* Karl Tate states, "In quantum physics, entangled particles remain connected so that actions performed on one, affect the other, even when separated by great distances. The phenomenon so riled Albert Einstein he called it 'spooky action at a distance'" (Tate, 2013).

The idea that two entities are so connected, even at great distances, that they can tremendously affect one another is a Fourth Density phenomenon. Assume the two entities are people. Say you are living in Australia, and your best friend is living in Canada. According to 4D quantum laws, when you have a strong experience, your best friend may sense the same strong feeling at the same time. If you have a car accident, she will feel a jolt. If you fall over sick, she will have a sick feeling. She will KNOW these feelings are connected to you, and you may get a phone call from her pretty quickly.

Telepathy works by this principle and arises in 4D as an everyday occurrence. Psychometry, telekinesis, precognition, and so many more "superpowers" are based on quantum entanglement. In Fourth Density, we become aware of our interconnectedness, and we begin to behave as if we are not detached, but very much attached. It is humanity's first baby-step into Unity: that we are all One Being.

As we move past the threshold of Fourth Density into Fifth Density and beyond, we'll watch spirituality and science merge into one. Everything you thought you knew about science will eventually be proven inadequate, as new shocking scientific fact overwrites the old. That's the fun part!

The Experience of Time in the Fourth Soul Level

We know that time and space are correlated. Einstein proved it with his theory of relativity. Let's explore what this concept can teach us about our experience in each density.

As your soul moves along through the densities, one after the next, it picks up momentum. The further you climb upwards in your personal consciousness, more thoughts occur in each moment. This is what causes the feeling that time is speeding up – because you are evolving at a faster and faster rate of speed.

As your consciousness expands, it moves closer and closer to the speed of light. **As you approach the speed of light, you have the EXPERIENCE of MORE HAPPENING within each moment.** Relative time slows down as we get closer to light speed, but it feels to you like more experiences are packed into each second. When you move closer to light-speed you have the ability to perceive more, think more and feel more during a given fragment of time. In 4D, you'll learn to use your consciousness to EXPAND an instant, to stretch it out. Doing so provides you with an opportunity to savor all that the moment contains.

Think of snow falling. Even in our current 3D state, snow appears to fall slowly. We have time to watch each snowflake as it descends. We have time to get to know what each flake looks like. It's a beautiful experience to feel a personal relationship to each snowflake. This kind of prolonged perception creates a *stillness within* that enables us to slow our minds and hearts. **It gives us time to catch up with ourselves.** Maybe that's why most folks like to watch falling snow - it produces a feeling of peacefulness. Peacefulness happens when we slow down long enough to catch up with what's going on inside. Peacefulness happens when we let ourselves be present in the eternal moment. It provides us space to integrate each nuance. It provides us time to process our thoughts and emotions.

You may have had a glimpse of "slowing down time" while meditating. Stillness fell upon your mind and body. You had a "peak experience" giving you a taste of what was to come when you reached Fourth Density (and beyond). These experiences are real gifts, and VERY different from the hustle-bustle 3Ders are used to. In 4D, every experience feels like watching falling snow. There's time to process and catch up with yourself. Overwhelm is seldom felt, even though so much more information is coming at you all the time.

As we move into higher stations on our Soul Map, we learn at a faster and faster rate of speed because WE HAVE MORE TIME. Our ability to take in information increases exponentially. Einstein seems to have been aware of all of this.

There's a great example of how humans are changing to take in information at shocking rates of speed. Let's swing back to the present day, 3D world for a moment. People younger than the age of approximately 30 years can multi-task like no human ever before. Because of the internet and social media, they are accustomed to taking in large quantities of information very quickly. (The internet is a 4D phenomenon.) You may also notice their ability to hold several abstract ideas in their minds at a time. These capabilities are presenting at far younger ages than ever before. Even though the shift hasn't completed itself yet, **some of the new-model-kids are fourth-density activated from birth.** Even if you're older – it's possible that you might have been born like this too.

Currently, more people are being born *wired for Fourth Density*.

If you, as Aurora, were able to time-travel back 250 years and visit your ancestors, you would appear to them as though you were glowing. That's how much your body's vibrational rate has increased in the higher worlds.

Time-lag

In the last chapter we discussed the Third Density time-lag between an idea and its fruition. However, in fully shifted Fourth Density, you will notice a much shorter time-lag. The ability to quickly manifest whatever you wish is a long-awaited super-power!

You'll begin mastering your skills of the Law of Attraction in earnest. It will be MUCH easier to learn to regulate your emotional and cognitive states in an attempt to manifest something you want or need. The full experience of 4D is more like a dream-world than anything you've ever known before. In dreams, we can manifest things instantaneously. It's very much like that in 4D. Plans take very little time to execute. Ideas are multidimensional and abstract, and can come into being rapidly.

In your incarnation as Aurora, you really enjoy being able to think of something you need, and have it appear very quickly. You, and everyone in Fourth Density, have everything you need because your consciousness has learned to control the spastic mind. **A controlled mind and calm heart can do what the busy mind and tortured heart cannot do.** Manifestation is swift because Aurora has *proven to the Universe that she can be trusted* with the superpower. Until your being shows the Universe that it is trustworthy, you won't have much success with manifestation - no matter how many vision boards you make.

Money and Work in the Fourth Soul Level

If you've heard of the Contributionism Movement, then you'll understand the concept of the way things will work in Fourth Density around money, trade, currency and work. You can learn more about Michael Tellinger's "Ubuntu" movement by going to the website: www.ubuntuplanet.org.

Michael Tellinger has said, "We are creating a totally new system, free from economic slavery, where we turn competition into collaboration. A new social structure where we all benefit from our collective efforts and individual talents. A new world where people are put before profits, and the resources & materials are used to enrich all our lives. Welcome to the world of UBUNTU and Contributionism" (Tellinger, 2012).

In 4D, you won't have to work - unless you want to. And you will want to - because contributing to the community is a completely fulfilling thing to do. When you do work, it may not pay you a salary. The work you do will help sustain everyone. Everyone will do what they can, and will do what they love.

How will this function? The system works because the hearts of 4Ders like Aurora will have opened so wide that service to others is the main driving force. Back in Third Density, Adam was focused on storing up as many assets as possible, forcing himself to ignore others (and his own sensitive feelings) in the process. Aurora and her friends know that the old ways are ineffective at best, and selfish at worst. They know that a system of contribution flows so much better. Why? **Because the 4D system is built on *trusting that EVERYONE has each other's back.***

Religion and Spirituality in the Fourth Soul Level

---

*"At every step of evolution,
man's realization of God changes.*
~ Hazrat Inayat Khan, Sufi Master

Entering Fourth Density will awaken your awareness enough to see God in a new way. Man-made religion will suddenly seem unfulfilling, shallow and far too binding. You'll probably begin to call yourself "spiritual, not religious" at this point. Although many people will stick with their beloved religions, they'll see them in a much deeper, more open way. In 4D, you'll be ready to expand into a whole new ability to feel the Divine. Before, Divinity was just a concept, but in Fourth Density, Divinity can be touched by the deeper soul. God will be experienced. Love, peace, mercy, forgiveness, justice and freedom for the entire world will become deeply held values.

In 4D, God will be seen as a loving, compassionate Creator, no longer as a judging, condemning father in the sky. Mankind's sense of morality will have evolved. It will be based on kindness, fairness, and compassion for all living beings.

Spiritual Awakening into the level of the heart will feel like a sudden sense of immense love and intimacy with God, your friends, yourself, and all that is. It will be an exquisite experience of emotional openness! Your willingness for goodwill toward others will expand outward to all beings everywhere, as you come to realize that all people's needs matter equally.

**Spiritual Awakening in Fourth Density is
the moment we fall in love with the world.
It's the moment we fall in love with God.
It's the moment the world becomes SAFE.**

Empaths in the Fourth Soul Level

Fourth Density is the natural home of the "Empath." Instead of sympathizing like you did in 3D, it's possible to feel into other people's hearts, and into their experiences. You'll literally feel what they feel.

If you are one of the rare people who is heart-activated here and now in 3D, life on Earth is probably painful for you. If you're living with a Fourth Density consciousness in a Third Density body, you have abilities beyond those of most people. It probably feels like being an alien in an alien world. **Interactions between an empath and a 3Der may seems like sandpaper to the empath's heart.** 3Ders don't know how to love unconditionally (even if they think they do). Their whole attitude toward life is different than the empath's. Empaths are naturally activating their heart-wisdom that knows what love is and how it behaves.

If you're reading this book, you're probably an empath or a 4Der living on 3D Earth just waiting for things to change! Trust yourself. You're here for a very important reason. Your job isn't necessarily to teach people, or become a guru, or even a devotee. Your real job as an empath is to DO YOUR OWN CLEARING WORK. As you focus on your own healing, wounds will clear for others as well. Be the silent example. Don't talk about what you know unless someone asks. **It would be an infringement of another**

person's free-will to tell them spiritual concepts they're not ready to hear. Until they ask, just let them be.

If you are currently an empath with your heart-chakra activated, just hold on a little longer. It's important that you protect yourself in a very tender way. Find like-hearted people to talk to. Try not to take the world on your shoulders (because it will completely wear you out). Keep a safe distance from mean people. Learn more and more about Who You Are and why you are different from the majority of humans. Get support from other empaths. (If you're interested, I moderate a closed group on Facebook for empaths. Search *"Paige Bartholomew's Support Group for Emerging Empaths"*).

Right now you're living as a heart-activated being in a 3D world. When you enter into your Fourth Density world, you'll finally feel like you're home. Comfort will be all around you. Relationships will feel MUCH safer. You'll no longer have to worry if someone will understand you, because most everyone will!

I appreciate your tremendous desire to help. I empathize with how much it hurts to watch as humanity seems to destroy itself. Have faith that NOTHING CAN BE DESTROYED, it can only be changed for the better.

The Road Narrows

When empaths begin to awaken, they may find long-term relationships suddenly ending, fewer like-minded friends, and loneliness. This happens because you will have up-leveled in a spiritual way, and there are fewer Earth humans who will resonate with you. It's a really hard change, but the Universe is asking awakening empaths to learn to lean on themselves and their internal and higher guidance. Looking for validation "out there" won't satisfy, and it won't answer your questions. The native

3Ders "out there" don't know the answers you're seeking. They may not even understand why you're questioning the status quo at all.

An empath often feels frustrated with other people because they don't see life as he sees it. He feels they mis-attune to him; they miss his intentions completely. He feels they don't understand him.

Doing Your Work

How do you get the healing done at the green light ray (4D) level? You must *accept* others as they are, try to *know them* to the best of your ability, and *love them* fully. You must *accept yourself* for not being perfected yet. You must *take responsibility* for your actions and *make amends* when appropriate. You must cry, write, or talk it through until you understand what's blocking the love within you. **This is the work the empath does in the world. It is your purpose.**

If the feelings are difficult to transform quickly, one thing the empath must do is to protect himself from spiraling. He knows he must keep himself focused inside, where the actual work goes on. **He knows he mustn't splay himself all about, spewing emotion like a wild garden hose.** He is aware that doing so would compromise his energetic/emotional field - and upset others. The empath makes a conscious choice to contain his wisdom-practice within, and to share it mainly with God. Sometimes a trusted other can be brought in for help. But the empath only chooses those who are capable of understanding his station. The empath never gives his Truth or his heart to someone who cannot see who he is.

In these ways, the empath transmutes emotion through his heart. He creates a space with God, for God, inside himself where he can work with everything that comes up. He leans on trustworthy friends who also possess 4D consciousness or above. He learns to become bigger than his feelings.

Used correctly, love dissolves distorted emotion.

Illusions and Struggles Experienced in the Fourth Soul Level

As beautiful as you will become as a 4Der, there will still be veils of illusion and misthought here.

"Love without Wisdom is Martyrdom."
~ The Law of One

Honoring your "Yes" as well as your "No"

In Fourth Density, you'll still only be about halfway through your journey of remembering. You'll be so full of tenderness for everyone and everything in this density that you'll sometimes forget your own needs. Sacrificing oneself for someone else isn't balanced and it isn't mastery. Fourth-ray boundaries look like this: Sometimes love means saying "no" in a way that honors yourself AND another. Doing so is not failing to love another. The ability to stay in love absolutely while saying "no" is a very equalizing, noble and advanced accomplishment.

If you know that you need to say no to something, but in doing so, you'll be infringing on the free-will of another person, the answer is RE-NEGOTIATION. If you must leave a job, a marriage, a partnership, or any commitment, it is your duty to yourself and to the other person to re-negotiate the agreement before you make any moves to change it. There is almost always a way to make things feel mutually beneficial. It is possible to meet both people's needs without compromising, betraying, breaking a contract, or breaking a heart. The fourth-density-activated human knows he must do it this way in order to become a master of love.

Imbalanced Love is like a wagon missing a wheel. Another veil you may experience in 4D is that you'll be so fully immersed in learning about loving, you might not even think about how wisdom might play into the picture. Love is incomplete without wisdom to balance it. You'll be working hard, learning all the facets of unconditional love; you'll be working lopsided without wisdom – like a cat with three legs. 4D doesn't teach you about wisdom. **Lessons on wisdom are coming soon as we study Fifth Density.**

Victimhood in 4D is a limitation which must be cleaned up. In the heart, there can be a negative tendency to see oneself as a victim. Yes, you already dealt with the problem of victim-mentality in 3D, but victimhood in the level of the heart is a more subtle form of feeling ineffective. There is a sense of frustration with the inability to see EVERYTHING yet. You'll want to know everything, and that can be exasperating. Because your soul will be trying to figure out how it fits in with Universal Power, confusion about that divine power will present itself in many ways. Of course the confusion is a catalyst for your growth. You must work through confusion until you figure out that **it's impossible to be a victim in a Universe in which you have been gifted co-Creatorship.**

How you feel is your choice. Remember the day your soul was born? It was gifted free-will, amnesia, and creative power. All of this time, you've been working to uncover that power, feeling afraid, out of control and mixed up. It seemed like circumstances were beyond your control. It seemed like you had to just accept things as they were, even if you didn't like it. It appeared that you had very little control over your own emotions, over outside influences, over humanity. A huge developmental milestone in the Fourth Density realm is the moment one wakes up to know that she has the power to feel and experience anything she prefers. Willingness to feel both comfortable and uncomfortable feelings is up to you. Your power lies in your choice to be present with everything as it appears – painful and joyful. Your power lies in accepting it all within your heart.

You have powers you didn't realize you had. In the Wizard of Oz, Dorothy possessed her power all along – in the last place she ever thought to look! Her shoes. Similarly, God placed your power in the last place you ever thought to look. It was not to be found in your ability to manipulate your outer circumstances, nor in rationalizing things through, nor through the use of logic, nor in avoiding or hiding, not even through loving. God placed your power within your higher illuminated consciousness. In late Fourth Density, your soul will see so much more of the Truth about how creation works. One of the greatest lessons in 4D is to develop the ability to cast off feelings of doubt, powerlessness and victimhood. You'll step into the knowledge of your true co-creative abilities. It will be a happy time.

Do not worry about any limitations or difficulties that you're bound to experience in Fourth Density. It's the natural way of things. By the time you're ready to cross over the energetic portal to Fifth Density, you'll have mastered the curriculum of the heart to the fullest degree. It all happens in perfect sequence.

.

The Path is Encoded

The entire curriculum required for Fourth Density is encoded into the fourth heart chakra. How does it guide you? The fourth chakra naturally provides inner yearnings and subconscious drives which motivate you toward completing the lessons you need to learn. These yearnings and drives will compel you to *feel into* everything. You might experience a natural interest to know your neighbor more deeply. You may experience a natural impulse toward helping the environment. You might feel a natural desire to contribute to social reform that helps underprivileged people. Your heart chakra will give you a strong desire to be a better person by becoming more authentic, more truthful, and more honest. Your heart chakra will give you deeper sensitivity to others' pain, where you will feel a strong yearning to help. The heart will lead you exactly where you need to go because **each chakra is like a living computer containing a built-in GPS. It happens like this for every soul, in every density. The chakras ignite strong feelings that encourage souls to learn the lessons they need at that moment. Listen to your impulses and instincts. The curriculum built into your fourth chakra will speak to you through these yearnings and drives, and show you where to go.**

The feeling you'll experience spiritually in Fourth Density is pure freedom compared to anything you've ever encountered before. Many people want to stop and linger here in their soul growth because of how good it feels. However, this place is not the end of your journey. At a certain point, you will start feeling unsatisfied. You must continue your evolution toward the "Soul Consciousness" of 5D.

What Aurora learned: Summing up the Fourth Soul Level

In your incarnations as Aurora, you spent many lifetimes in 4D practicing living from the heart. By the end of your tour through Fourth Density, you've learned what it's like to drop the need to "be right," You've learned to participate in authentic communication and true connection with another. You did your work to purify lower emotion. You're no longer at the mercy of your emotions because you learned what they really are, and how to use them properly. **We never get rid of our feelings.** In fact, we never get rid of ANYTHING in all our travels throughout the Soul Map. We simply come to understand everything as it truly exists in Reality, in its original state of Truth, the way it was created on the first day. Your veils drop away, and you become a master of Fourth Density Love.

During your many lifetimes in 4D, you, as Aurora, learned how to meet others heart-to-heart and to let the mind take a back seat. You loosened your attempts at self-protection so that you could be free to open into real intimacy with yourself and others. Once you, as Aurora, didn't have to spend so much time and energy protecting yourself, or making money to survive, you found that you had loads more time to spend on interesting endeavors, compassionate relationships, and whatever pastimes brought you joy. You let go of your grip, surrendered, and expanded yourself into Universal Love. Aurora fell in love with all that is.

The Last Task for the Fourth Soul Level: Shifting into 5D

Sorting through the subtle veils of 4D will help you open your heart so wide that all emotion is neutralized. When this happens, you've mastered love and emotion. When you open your mind so broadly you can finally realize the startling truth: **you had the ruby slippers all along.** You will come to know that you had power and CHOICE over all that you experienced.

The last action step in Fourth Density which will get you through the 4D gateway is to **give up expectations of any sort.** This has to be total, so if you're going to meditate on one thing — let SURRENDERING YOUR EXPECTATIONS be the focus. Giving up wanting things brings instant peace. Your longing heart thinks it knows how to manage things for you. It is misinformed. Surrender wanting love or comfort, or for things to go your way. Give up believing that if you pray hard enough, or try hard enough to manifest your vision boards, you'll get what you think you want. Only your highest self knows what you really need. Wanting anything except what your higher self wants for you will bring disappointment, frustration, pain and despair.

Each day, meditate on giving up the desire for your relationships to be any certain way, wishing your body felt different than it does, or any sort of wishing. ACCEPTING WHAT IS HERE may feel counter-intuitive to manifesting the life you want. You may think that surrendering means giving up. This is a narrow understanding. Surrender is the highest form of bowing your lower self in reverence to your higher knowing. **Letting go of what you think you want, is the first step to getting what you want – because it immediately puts you in a position to have what you need.**

Then, your inner Soul Map can take over from there.

When we reach the threshold of each new density, the last, and most vital task is always surrender. Give leadership back to the part of us that is in union with God.

Our ultimate goal is to know that Love is the only thing that's real. Everything else is unreal. None of it matters. Start living this way now. After much practice, when your natural, go-to action is to "accept what is," you'll be ready to swing into the realm of unlimited consciousness. Then you'll be ready to cross the threshold into Fifth Density.

Move into impersonal love.
Surrender all of your neediness.
Open your heart to be shown
something you've never known.
This is the doorway to Fifth Density.

Chapter 10

The Fifth Level of Soul Evolution

Wisdom
or
"The Illuminated Intellect"

"Wisdom is not cleverness, but infinitely superior to it.
Wisdom works independently of the physical means,
and therefore, requires intuition.
The clever person works by means of his physical body,
but the wise person works independently of it."
~ Hazrat Inayat Kahn

Shifting from 4D to 5D means making a qualitative change in understanding yourself beyond the physical you. **The primary developmental task in this level of consciousness is to master the realm of your soul.** It is at this level of consciousness that you will begin to access true wisdom. You'll finally be able to combine everything you've learned from the lower four densities and merge it into a more complete understanding of who you REALLY are and the Truth of your existence.

We have two intellectual capacities: logic, which is the 3D way of thinking, and wisdom, which is the 5D way of thinking. In Third Density, intellectual capacity is referred to as the "lower intellect;" and in Fifth Density intellectual capacity is referred to as the "illuminated intellect." The illuminated intellect is also called "wisdom." In Third Density you are only capable of a lower form of thought, and therefore you are limited in your intellectual ability. In Fifth Density you are capable of a higher form of thought, and therefore you possess a greater capacity for truth-finding.

You will continue to build on everything you've ever learned: physical instinct (1D), emotional instinct (2D), personal will (3D), loving compassion (4D), and now you'll begin to learn a new and expanded part of yourself - **knowing**. It's what the Sufis call "certainty." Spiritual seeking will no longer be necessary because knowing has taken its place. You will have the ability to reach into the quantum field and pull out the answers you need. When you graduate from a 4D heart-centered body to a 5D light body, your compassionate nature will remain, but a new component will be added into the mix: **the capacity to discern truth from falsehood.**

Encoded in your fifth chakra are the tools you need to learn about the following attributes:

- Learning to tell the truth with absolute honesty,
- Discernment for what is true and what is untrue,
- Wisdom for how to behave, speak, balance relationships,

and to use truth and love in an integrated way,
- Deeper insight into the reality of why you behave the way you do, and why others behave the way they do,
- Being with relationships in a new way,
- Facing whatever comes in the present moment for yourself and other,
- Learning to live without expectations.

The Experience of the Fifth Soul Level

Fifth Density will be your first experience of living in a spiritual world. Densities one through three were tightly compressed worlds where you were learning about yourself through physicality. Fourth Density was a bridge-world where you used both your body and the love in your heart to walk upon your spiritual path in order to open new and wonderful spaces within. Densities five through seven are the "spiritual worlds," or "Worlds of Light."

When you cross through the gate to Fifth Density, you'll experience a sudden, breathtaking understanding of non-linearity, multi-dimensionality, and the many vast planes of the non-physical. You'll move from your previous consciousness (Fourth Density) where a blend of intuition and love was the modus operandi, into a new operating system. A fresh sense has awakened within you: **your "truth-ometer,"** which you will use as your primary sensing tool. Your truth-ometer is innately capable of discerning Universal Truth from untruth, which is an enormous gift! Your truth-ometer has never been activated during all your previous incarnations. You may have had some capacity to feel truth reverberating through your being before, but this is different. At the level of 5D, you'll KNOW the truth naturally. You'll move from focusing on content (3D), and feeling (4D), into a much truer Reality (5D). **You won't see things objectively OR**

subjectively anymore. You'll begin to see things neutrally – just as they are. You'll begin to see TRUTH just as it is.

The primary developmental task throughout your experience here in 5D is to *master accurate spiritual discernment which leads to Wisdom*. The action step to be mastered in 5D is "trust." This isn't the same kind of trust you worked with in 3D or 4D. This is a kind of trust which is developed for the Self, by the Self, without need for any outer validation. It is ultimately experienced as a complete trust in your Higher Self and your ability to communicate with the Universe itself. In 5D, for the first time, the satisfaction of knowing TRUTH, and a feeling of abiding PEACE is possible.

Fifth Density corresponds to the fifth chakra in the body and the "blue light ray" on the visible spectrum. The fifth, or throat chakra, is located in the mid-neck area. (A reminder: your chakras exist in your energy body. They are present whether you possess a physical body or not. So even here in your 5D light body, your throat chakra is in exactly the same spot as it would be in your physical body.) Many people think that because we're working within the guidance system of the throat chakra, it means the main lesson has something to do with speech or communication, which isn't the full picture. **The fifth chakra carries, among other important lessons, the way to teach you to discern reality from "irreality."**

There will be a sudden change in how you see togetherness. In 3D, you saw each person, place, and thing as separate. Your Third Density concept was "both/and." There was a separate thing, plus another separate thing – and those equaled two separate things. Conversely, in Fifth Density, you'll see things as binary. Dictionary.com defines the word binary as "a whole composed of two." It sounds paradoxical that two separate things are now seen as one whole. Although it's paradoxical to the human mind, it's not to the higher mind. The higher Fifth Density mind understands paradoxes perfectly! The Fifth Density mind LIVES FOR PARADOX!

You will have much to learn during your time in Fifth Density. In order to truly understand your soul, you must come to a clear recognition of reality *as it is* - not as you perceive it or want it to be. **ACCEPTANCE is the tool which allows you to see what's real.** Radical acceptance of everything exactly as it is without preference or personal agenda provides a perfect picture of reality.

Everything that appears in 5D comes into being by a powerful combination of **Love combined with Consciousness.** Heart wisdom presents as unconditional, divine love. Fifth Density mystical-mind-wisdom presents as light. The combination is called "Love/Light." This term is used by the authors of The Law of One book series (Elkins, 1984).

I invite you to imagine, with eyes closed, living full-time in a World of Light. I invite you to imagine a love so un-veiled that you're able to feel the exquisite essence of everything and everyone you come into contact with. What does that feel like? Imagine trusting yourself so completely that you know everything about yourself. Imagine no more confusion, and no more uncertainty. Imagine being able to reach into the Source Field and pull out bits of information, anytime you need them. Imagine being able to download cosmic knowledge whenever you want to. Imagine honing your power of creation so that you are able to experience whatever circumstances are most useful to you. Imagine feeling free from physical pain, free from emotional turmoil, and free from drama. Imagine feeling free enough to pursue your bliss every moment of your life. This is just a small taste of what Fifth Density is like.

Our heart is how we feel all the things we can't see.

When we integrate the power of imagination with the love and

strength of our heart, our world will change.

~ Nasim Haremein

The Fifth Density Kit

When you incarnate into any density, you receive a special suit to wear. Your kit is comprised of three parts: a physical body, an emotional body, and a mental body. Each time you advance to a higher density, you'll get an upgraded kit.

Your Physical Light Body Kit

Once you have learned enough, you will pass through the Fifth Density gateway. Then you'll experience everything as a very high level of light. Your body will reflect this change. You'll live in **a body of light within a World of Light**. There is still a certain degree of matter but it's not the kind you know here in 3D. It may make it easier to understand if you think of this matter as something like plasma.

Communication is no longer accomplished by talking with your mouth. It's all telepathic here because 5Ders understand quantum science. Remember when we discussed the idea of time seeming to speed up? When your being vibrates near light speed more thoughts get packed into each moment of time. Thoughts come so fast in 5D, it would take days just to communicate one whole thought with words. Telepathy is a faster way to communicate. Whole chunks of comprehension can be transmitted in seconds. Understanding between two people can be conveyed in giant downloads. **Pictures, symbols, geometry, color, sound, and feeling combine to make "thought bombs."** These thought bombs can be transmitted from person to person through the mind. This kind of communication is impeccably accurate!

In 5D you will leave the physical environment altogether. You'll live in a world of energy, with energy bodies, energy food, energy earth, energy plants and animals, energy homes, etc.... Everything will be non-physical for the first time. Spend some time just imagining how life as we know it will change!

Your Mental Kit

Fifth Density beings use an advanced form of thought, completely unimaginable to lesser-evolved humans. Once you graduate into 5D, you'll naturally blend all of the learning you've mastered into a whole new way of thinking. You'll combine your knowledge about primal existence (1D), emotions (2D), reason (3D), intuition (4D), and now you'll add something even more refined into the mix: **holographic conceptualization.** Using all of these skills at once will give you the ability to think on a higher level than you ever conceived of before. Creativity will go through the roof. The rapidity at which you will be able to think will astound you. You'll be able to hold hundreds of pieces of information in your mind. You will be able to see a picture so big you can cannot even conceive it yet.

Tolle describes the 3D spastic mind that speaks at approximately 45 words per minute – to itself. In Fifth Density, you will be learning to master your higher intellect so that the mind is used as a refined instrument. You will learn to still the mind, to control it, and to use much more of it toward positive purpose.

Did you know that Third Density brains only use 5 to 10 percent of their capacity? FIVE TO TEN PERCENT. What if you could use fifty percent? Or seventy-five percent? That's what will happen as you grow in spiritual development. In 5D, you are learning to use more and more of your consciousness. The mind is waking up! Just think about the possibilities! What would it be like to live in a world where everyone was using even 50 – 75 percent of their brains? Wow.

"The mind is a superb instrument...

If used RIGHTLY.

Used wrongly,

it becomes very destructive.

It is not so much that you use your mind wrongly,

you usually do not use it all.

IT USES YOU."

~Eckhart Tolle

Your Emotional Kit

Fifth Density will mark the beginning of your journey into the upper realms of the "adult soul." Once a soul is ready to cross over the threshold into 5D, it must leave all the games behind. White lies, small manipulations, harboring even small amounts of hidden jealousy, projection, pride, resentment, and the like are what I call "game-playing." Children play emotional games. Children hold onto grudges and act them out because there's a payoff for them. Adult souls in 5D are willing to sit face-to-face with themselves. They accept responsibility for themselves and they accept reality as it is. Because you'll finally see that all the worlds are made of thought-energy, you will realize that you are *responsible for your circumstances.* Adult souls are able and willing to put all of the self-deception behind them.

Once a soul is ready to live in Fifth Density, there can be no more games. Scrupulous, transparent honesty with one's self is required. Without it, one simply cannot even enter Fifth Density!

What does it mean that one "can't" enter Fifth Density? As I mentioned before, the veil between densities operates on vibrational frequency. **It can only let those souls through who have _come to be_ the same frequency of the gateway.** Everything carries a frequency. An act of dishonesty carries a low frequency. An act of honesty carries a high one, allowing a soul to cross the threshold into 5D.

Passing through the veil between densities is always a matter of resonance.

If your vibrational resonance has evolved to the corresponding gateway frequency, you'll effortlessly make the shift to the other side and enter into 5D with grace and ease. If your resonance still isn't high enough, you'll stay put in 4D. This is true for every level of consciousness, in every density.

The Sufis say that a person has to travel through the "eye of a needle" in order to move on to the next world. The eye of the needle represents the gateway between densities. The saying means that you have to become willing to shed everything but your essential self in order to pass through. Check your emotional response to what you just read. It may feel scary, or it may seem exciting! Your emotional response can be used as a clue to reveal your current level of readiness. If the idea of throwing your ego off like an old cloak and taking on a new adventure excites you, then you are probably ready for a higher level of growth (or are already there)! If it feels scary, then you still have more work to do right where you are. And that's perfectly ok! **But don't shirk the work!** Keep trying and keep moving.

The information you learn about yourself from reading this book will help you to know where you are and where you're going. It will also help you get a general sense of the levels at which your friends and family resonate. Again, I encourage you not to <u>ever</u> use any insight about yourself as a way to compare yourself to others, or as a weapon with which to beat yourself up, or as a way to judge others. Use the insights you glean from this book as information to help you. Do your best to practice being grateful for where you are, for WHO you are, and especially you being given the opportunity to be the camera lens for God! The more grateful you can be for your present circumstances, the faster you'll sail through the stations.

An Incarnation in the Fifth Soul Level

Let's imagine you've just been born into a brand new lifetime in a 5D world. Your parents name you Celestia. Beings are "born" from parents in Fifth Density, but since bodies are only energy and no longer dense matter, the process is somewhat different. **It takes a conscious CHOICE on the part of all three beings to bring the child through the birth veil - the child, the mother and the father.** Birth is an energetic accomplishment where your soul travels from the astral realm before birth to the desired world you want to join. Each party (parents and child) participate in the decision-making before conception and throughout the birthing process. This is actually true of birth in EVERY density – the difference in 5D is that everyone is *conscious* of the process.

You, as Celestia, have a beautiful spirit-body. It is made of light, color, awareness and love, and it has abilities beyond imagining! **Your body can travel at the speed of thought.** You won't need a bike, a car, a train, a plane or a spaceship because travel will be a function of your consciousness - even space and time-travel. All experiences will be a function of your mind. If you want to go visit your Auntie Viola, all you will have to do is think about her, transmit a telepathic request for permission to come over (because all things must be agreed upon between people in 5D), and you'll suddenly appear at her house!

People live in houses in 5D. They also live in palaces, castles, caves, huts, bubbles, crystals, and on top of clouds! People live where they like. All the dwellings are built with thought. No construction is needed! Everywhere you look, you will see things which are built by someone's imagination and creativity. The Fifth Density world is beautiful beyond measure.

Envision what a house made of energy would look like. Is it sparkly? Transparent? Solid? Fluid? Does it sit on the very edge of a cliff, hanging out over the sea? Does it float on air? With your imagination, you have the power to instantly make your house pink one day, then change it to white with blue shutters the next day. Maybe, instead of glass, your windows are made of filmy soap bubbles, or an energy field! Maybe the walls are made of living trees - twisted trunks and branches create a conscious house that knows you, and perhaps work WITH you in perfect concert! You are only limited in what you can create with your own imagination!

Celestia's body has become energy, too. Imagine what your body looks like in 5D? Since you have the ability to create whatever you want, you can make your body solid or intangible at will. Maybe you like to fly! Maybe you like to breathe underwater! You can do anything you choose with your body – because of its

145

energetic nature, and because of the level of your expanded consciousness. Its fun to think about, isn't it?

For Celestia, all of this is just normal everyday life. She's living in harmony with the plants growing in her garden, and in return, those plants give her the gift of beautiful flowers and fruit. Because she understands them, they know exactly how to feed and nourish her in return. Colors are more vibrant than you had ever seen in Third Density. Celestia sees hundreds of colors that 3D humans are incapable of sensing with their physical eyes. Colors far to the lower end of the spectrum, or infrared, and colors far to the higher end of the spectrum, or ultraviolet, are perceivable. **Celestia sees *hues in between hues.*** The whole world is so bright that it would *blind* a physical, 3D human. Every sight you see in 5D induces vibrancy in the heart. Celesia's Fifth Density world keeps her feeling happy and inspired wherever she goes.

Social Consciousness in the Fifth Soul Level

When you lived in Fourth Density, compassion was the name of the game. You learned that when you stepped on someone else, it injured YOU. Fourth Density was the time when your heart became fully functional – you were suddenly able to see that everyone else mattered as much as you did - no one was higher, no one was lower.

In Fifth Density, you will begin to learn the mysteries of the soul. With direct soul-to-soul connection, your view of yourself and others will again change. Imagine being so close to other people that you can hear their thoughts, feel their feelings, and merge with their light bodies (with permission, of course.) What occurs societally in 5D is so much more than simply cooperation or collaboration. People are so deeply joined together that social projects work seamlessly with very little negotiation. Yes, you will still have a separate self at this level, and you may want to do some creative projects on your own. Even then, your contributions are considered gifts to all, and are deeply honored in every way – because others know that without you, society could not function. It is well understood that each and every person is a vital part of the whole, and that the very universe could not run without each one.

How would you feel if you could know that you mattered to every single person on Earth? They all saw you, knew you, and appreciated all of your contributions? You would no longer feel alone. You would feel loved, included, and secure.

In 5D, survival needs will be met for everyone. You all worked SO VERY HARD for this in 4D! You dreamed of a utopia like this one, and you made it. Because of your personal growth and your efforts, you and your friends will create this heavenly world.

Religion and Spirituality in the Fifth Soul Level

In your Fifth Density incarnation as Celestia, you're beginning see your Creator in a new way. Man-made religions of old will seem like children's bedtime stories. You're finding out that not only are you able to merge with other people, but you're learning to merge with the Divine itself! Here in 5D, Celestia's heart will swell with the knowing that she and the Creator are much less separated than she could see before, although her understanding of Oneness is still somewhat incomplete. That's ok. Complete re-merging with the Creator won't occur fully until the end of Seventh Density.

Remember when you were still living in Fourth Density? You knew God as a loving, compassionate Creator, no longer as a judging, condemning father in the sky. Back then, in 4D, the morality of mankind evolved to a love-based experience, rooted in compassion, kindness and fairness.

**All spiritual growth is a
REMEMBERING PROCESS.
You don't "learn" spirituality. You uncover it.**

Your God of 3D, who doled out punishments and rewards, lived in your distant past. You'll come to know that God is the Creator of all that is, but that you (the creation) have the capability to decide what will come about for yourself. The Source of All Things sets everything into motion, but the creation (you) is in charge of its own destiny. Your world will be a perfect reflection of your purposeful, creative thoughts. As a 3Der and 4Der, you may have understood this law intellectually, but now, as a 5Der, it's experiential. It's IN YOU. You feel it and you live by it.

In 5D, you will no longer feel skepticism for "weird stuff," like ESP, levitation, remote viewing, accessing other realms, interstellar travel in "thought ships," seeing ghosts, spirits, angels, or higher-frequency beings. You, in 5D, will fully experience such paranormal events once you actually see the 5D world with your own eyes. You will have a complete understanding of how this "weird stuff" occurs.

You'll come to see that the paranormal is actually Reality. Telepathy, telekinesis, psychometry, clairaudience, clairsentience, clairvoyance, the ability to create material substance out of thin air will all be part of your normal daily life. Scientific understanding of the Source Field, otherwise known as "intelligent space," will be routinely taught in 5D school. Every child living in Fifth Density will be taught that matter is created from the universal vacuum, through the use of consciousness.

Spiritually emerging into the level of the soul feels like a sudden sense of Truth revealing itself to you. You'll understand everything: your friends, yourself, the basic laws of universal cosmology, who the prophets really are, who the E.Ts really are, the true meaning of "good" or "bad," and so much more. Wisdom will show you that, not only is your friend equal to you, but he is your inseparable co-Creator. People do not hurt one another in Fifth Density because when the wisdom of the 5th chakra is activated, one realizes that to hurt one individual *hurts everyone: ALL Beings Everywhere.* In all realms. In all levels. In all universes.

Science and Technology in the Fifth Soul Level

Newtonian physics was the science of the Third Density world. Quantum physics was the science of the Fourth Density world. Geometry is the science of the Fifth Density world.

Geometry is a living, moving, shifting consciousness which builds universes. It morphs and breathes in response to the will of the observer who wishes to create, using it as a tool. It is alive.

Fifth Density science is the science of the alive MIND. When you arrive in 5D, things will get really fun! Scientists will discover that all **materiality is created by consciousness,** and thereby can be *manipulated with* consciousness. In other words, you'll be able to create anything you wish, (using sacred geometry) as long as you are 5D activated!

In 3D, humans created mechanical machines to do work for them. In 4D, people discovered higher technologies based on quantum laws, like anti-gravity, free energy, food replicators, and the like. In Fifth Density, you'll be able to create what you need and want **through the natural power of your being** instead of through the clumsy use of technology. The higher mind "sees" in geometric patterns. You'll use this skill as a way to assemble reality like a three-dimensional puzzle (three dimensional means length, width, and depth). Because you will no longer be weighed down by the heaviness of dense physicality, you'll have the power to manifest anything you want or need.

What's the catch? By the time you move into Fifth Density consciousness – you won't want the same things you wanted in 3D, or even 4D. Not only that – but you'll be crafting your life like a Master by now. You no longer use colorful markers and big posters to make vision boards like you did in 3D. The idea of Third Density Laws of Attraction seem like child's play to you. In 4D, you used your Emotional Guidance Scale to attract physical matter and circumstances to you by way of emotional resonance. Even that system will seem elementary.

Nassim Haramein is a prominent physicist whose work is gaining notoriety. Since before Einstein, physicists have been searching for a single unifying principle that could knit Newtonian physics (3D) together with the quantum world (4D). Nassim Haramein appears to have discovered that unifying principle. Instead of looking for a particle at the source of all creation, Haramein looked for a fundamental *pattern* instead. Geometric patterns are the blueprints that build physical reality. Haramein naturally used his 5D latent memories to guide him to shocking theoretical solutions which most physicists have trouble answering. He was able to use his 5D superpowers to peer into the template world to view the geometric blueprint. He reasoned that if we can understand the fundamental geometric pattern that creates all things, we can work out how the entire universe is constructed. Can you see how multidimensional his thinking is? That's Fifth Density. Learn more from Haramein's Google Play documentary called Black Whole (Jensen, 2018).

Haramein did something unusual for a person in a 3D world. He had a lifelong vision of higher-realm-reality that held answers to his questions. He used the consciousness of 5D (his mystical-mind) to access the information he knew was hidden in the Fifth Density field. Haramein's personal genius is in using his *intuition* to explore, discover and learn! (It is my personal suspicion that Haramein possesses 5D or 6D consciousness while living in a Third Density body.)

He proved that the Source Field works with a fractalized pattern to produce the material universe, and he used geometry to figure it out. He calculated the mass of a square centimeter of empty space. Haramein theorizes that we are literally living on the inside of an enormous black hole. This is merely the beginning of a fascinating science which Fifth Density will fully reveal to humanity in time.

To learn more about Nassim Haramein's intriguing work, check out his website: www.resonancescience.org, or watch his compelling television series, *Quantum Revolution,* on Gaia TV (Haramein, 2004). Haramein has also authored a book called *Cosmometry* (Haramein, 2019).

What Lies Just Beyond the Event Horizon of our Current 3D Black Hole?

Each density is lying within the next, like nesting dolls. 1D lies inside 2D. 2D lies inside 3D. 3D lies inside 4D, etc. When we reach the end of our lessons in each level, we go through the gateway to a new density. These gateways are black holes where everything must disintegrate in order to be integrated anew on the other side. It doesn't hurt, and it isn't frightening to traverse through density gateways/black holes. It's a joyous experience.

In 5D, you'll understand that "what you live comes from what you are." Life is a hologram. What's on the inside shows up as a perfect replica on the outside. Your outer life is a perfect reflection of YOU, bursting outward for you to see in real time!

What a cool way to KNOW ONESELF. All you have to do is look at your life, and you'll see your blocks, your limitations, your intelligence, your creativity, your love! Everywhere you look, you see only yourself. The Sufis say, "Know yourself, and you'll know God." You're getting to know yourself deeply now, in fifth density, which means you're on the way to knowing God.

Only a highly developed being earns the right to wield these holy knowledges. It take a long time to slowly walk our way through the levels of the Soul Map in order to learn, step by step, to be in alignment with the One Creator. Remember, in order to pass through the energetic gateway to 5D you have to reach a vibrational level of personal integrity. You will literally be a different person than you were before. You will be very pure. With that purity, you will come to a deeper level of responsibility. Your willingness to become ultra-trustworthy, honest, free from selfish needs and desires – all of this is what will earn you the tremendous power you'll be holding in your hands in 5D. It would not be given to you any other way.

Once we all evolve enough to cross into Fifth Density, our planet will also cross over. At that time, the Earth will be a very, very different place than it seems today. **The science of physics will expand to such a degree that humans will learn to use the vacuum of space (the consciousness that resides behind and within sub-atomic particles) for everything we need.**

Love = Heart energy
Light = Wisdom energy
Sound = Propellant Vehicle

Love, light and sound (vibrations) are the basic instruments used to make all of creation – for both physical and non-physical worlds. Love, light and sound are the science of 5D. Living geometry is made of these. The living breath of geometry could be imagined as looking into a kaleidoscope. In Fifth Density you will finally become aware of how the creation works.

Time in the Fifth Soul Level

In your new fifth dimensional reality, time will seem fluid and less restrictive than before. In 3D, the world ran on clocks. In 5D, the world has shifted to such a spiritual way of living that timekeeping is no longer relevant. You just know where you're supposed to be and when.

Time is nothing like you thought it was in your limited 3D interpretation. **In Fifth Density, you'll live in "time/space" - the inverse of "space/time".** Linear time will no longer be perceived, unless one wants to go visit the filmstrip-like reality of lower densities.

One very cool new superpower Celestia finds for herself is slowing and speeding up time at will. She can travel to the past and to the future. But these timelines are different from the way most current physicists conceive of them today. 5D timelines are unlimited in number. They are fluid-like parallel realities that a conscious being may jump in and out of at will.

When you lived as Adam, in a 3D world, you could not understand these intricacies of the science of time. You didn't know that time and space are holographic and that both can easily be manipulated. Celestia finds life in Fifth Density so freeing! She stretches time as a tool for her own learning and her own personal enjoyment. Time has a natural consciousness to it. If a tear in the "fabric" of time occurs, time will repair itself. If a paradox accidentally forms, time will re-write itself to correct for the inconsistency. Of course, time is behaving in these ways consistently – not just in 5D. Humans don't grasp such abstract concepts until they've sufficiently evolved.

If you are comprehending immense abstractions of time and space right now, in the present, there may be a part of your mind that is tapping into fifth density knowledge via peak states. Or you may be a 5D Volunteer Soul. (See Volunteer Souls in Chapter 13.)

Time-Lag

Remember that annoying time-lag we had in 3D? The one where we used to have to wait for our thoughts to manifest? It's gone. In 5D, there is no time-lag. Whatever is thought of instantly becomes reality. **In Fifth Density you will begin learning to create WORLDS.** How's that for evolved?

Money, Currency and Work in the Fifth Soul Level

In your incarnation as Celestia, you don't have to work for money to sustain your life because you are capable of creating everything you need at every thought. Humanity in 5D collectively develops a society based on cooperation and sharing for the good of all beings everywhere. Money, and even bartering, are things of the past.

Back in Third Density, life used to be centered on working hard for one's physical survival. **In Fourth Density, humanity learned that everyone is equal, and that if we each give what we can, things WILL WORK TOGETHER FOR THE GOOD OF ALL.** In Fifth Density, beings have mastered love and equality so profoundly that physical survival is truly effortless. All things are made of energy, and 5Ders know how to *think reality into being*. This leaves plenty of time and personal vitality to explore the wonders of the self, other-selves and the extraordinary nature of the created universe.

You won't be expected to work in the same sense as before. You'll only be expected to do what you really love. And what 5Ders love to do the most is to create and to learn! How can that be a sustainable system? Here's how: 5Ders create their societies as a function of mind. You won't need food replicators, 3D printers, or other technologies here. Everything that's needed will be made available by the power of consciousness. Necessities are created using living geometry abundant in the source field. **When a need arises, the solution is apparent.** When everyone does what they love, everything flows, because most of the blocks to love that you used to carry have been dissolved. The blocks to love kept you stuck and unhappy. In Fifth Density, love flows. People living in 5D use their energy to love themselves, to serve community, to enjoy life, and to gain knowledge. They will continue to remember the secrets they forgot on the day the Creator gave birth to their souls. Remembering forgotten secrets is SO MUCH FUN! Fighting and struggling have ceased. There is only support for all people. Doesn't that sound absolutely beautiful?

Sex, Love and Relationships in the Fifth Soul Level

If you choose to engage in romantic partnership in 5D, you'll realize that your desires and needs are very different than they used to be. You'll no longer partner for economic stability, out of loneliness, or even to satisfy your sexual urges to procreate. Partnering will be fully conscious, with each party deeply knowing who they are, and who the other is. The coy, manipulative mating games of 3D will not seem interesting. You will no longer want to flirt or try to appear sexy to win a mate. These things will seem silly. The mating rituals of old were subtle forms of power and manipulation which Fifth Density folks do not take part in. They don't need to manipulate others to attract a wonderful partner. *Their partners arrive as a matter of matching resonance.*

Coupling won't be about playing with polarity anymore; it will be about exploring anew ability to *merge* with a partner. Love-making will become a spiritual practice where each partner releases his or her personal boundaries to *move into the other's being*. Perfect trust must be in place for this process to occur – and that's the evolutionary milestone of Fifth Density: **complete safety with each other.** You'll experience unblemished honesty, transparency, perfect communication and trust. If it were not so, merging with another soul would not be possible.

Back in 3D, you were working hard to create strong boundaries because they were necessary to know yourself as an individual, as well as to keep yourself safe. The downside to boundaries was that they not only kept the unwanted stuff out, but they also inadvertently *kept the good stuff out*, as well. Here in 5D, you've evolved to a point where you don't need those kinds of boundaries. Blending boundaries is desirable and pleasurable. *We first have to create boundaries (3D) before we develop a strong enough "sense of self" to let our boundaries down (4D and beyond).* This is why it takes so much TIME to evolve. We have to learn step by step. Blending boundaries is a blissful, joyful, strong and potent feeling. It's quite a relief to finally be able to relax into someone's heart and soul without fear that they might hurt you.

When Celestia chooses a mate (and her mate chooses her in return), the two simultaneously know that they will come together as a long-term, committed couple. Celestia and her mate do not play "hard to get" or other games, because in 5D, people can see right through each other! It's not fun, nor is it necessary to keep one's feelings hidden. **There are no secret thoughts.** It's a lot more fun to be in love with Love itself, and to share that Love with another being. In this way you allow the purifying nature of Love to work magic between two beings by opening their hearts and minds. Opening is what allows growth to occur. 5Ders enjoy growing and creating more than anything, and it's even more fun and effective to do it with a partner.

Sexuality is very different in this density, because beings are far less polarized between masculine and feminine. In 3D and 4D, people still need to explore yin/yang polarities, but not in 5D. Finally, the purpose for coupling is simply to *unite*. Beings are ready to do away with polarity. Uniting feels amazing when total trust is in place. Total trust occurs in Fifth Density because souls have purified any tendencies toward dishonesty, blocking their feelings, or withholding their hearts. People don't feel vulnerable in 5D. How could you feel vulnerable when you trust everyone to treat you with love and respect? All of that happens when we heal all of our blockages to love, and that's what Celestia and her partner have done.

The "Empath" transforms into the "Knower"

In 4D, empaths were invested in learning how to make things fair for all people. It was their main developmental task. Empaths did this through putting themselves in other people's shoes and empathizing with their situations.

In 5D, you'll have an extreme change of insight. Instead of seeing other people as "separate others" and using empathy to sense what they are feeling and thinking, **you now *join* with others to fully experience the way they are experiencing the moment.**

In 5D, you take a leap from empathy to KNOWING.

You'll no longer have to assume what others go through, you'll KNOW what they go through, because you will be able to seep into their field and experience the whole complex, extraordinary picture for yourself. This process takes great compassion and great confidence between two people. In 5D – it'll be your natural state.

The "Secret Worlds of Light"

Fifth Density is the first of the three Worlds of Light, otherwise called "the upper worlds". The Sufis call all of the knowledges here "secrets" because one cannot access them until he or she has attained a certain level of purity within. Hopefully, this book is giving you a *taste* of what these upper worlds are like. Having a sense of what's to come is very important for spiritual growth!

We, all souls, collectively created the seven-density Soul Map model for remembering who we really are. We created it with great care. We created the gateways between densities like secure airlocks. These airlocks only allow through that which resonates with the vibrational gateway. In the world of Fifth Density, one must be pure of heart, mind, and agenda before one is aligned with the gateway, and so, able to get in.

What is a "World of Light"? Light illuminates. Light shines on darkness and eradicates mis-thought. Therefore the Worlds of Light are places where shadows live no longer. In contrast to the harshness of the lower worlds, the upper worlds contain only Love, Understanding, Wisdom, Knowing, and Unification.

Once you enter into the Worlds of Light, you will begin your journey through the realms of angels. The upper worlds are where angels reside, and once you master these upper worlds, you will become an angel yourself.

If you knew now what you will eventually know in 5D, it would blow your mind. A 3D body cannot live at this level of light, as your physicality would disintegrate into nothingness by mere exposure to the vibration.

In Fifth Density, you will know the love of God personally. The Sufi's have a saying, "God is closer to you than your jugular vein." The multi-layered secrets of this statement will begin to unfold within you. In fact, all statements of Truth have multiple meanings which are revealed in ecstatic waves of recognition. 3D humans call these multiple meanings "paradoxes." However, once you evolve so far as Fifth Density, you will know in your deepest being that there is no such thing as a paradox. **Paradox is nothing more than layers of truth which unveil themselves, layer after layer, outside of the filmstrip of time.** From the perspective of a 3Der, paradoxes look like multiple seemingly divergent truths that shouldn't exist at the same time. They don't make sense! But that's because a 3Der isn't able to look outside of the filmstrip of time to see the way one sequence naturally leads into another, proving that all ideas DO make sense together. To a 3Der, a paradox looks illogical. In 5D, your mind will hold all of these meanings beautifully together in exquisite tapestry of certainty and bliss. These are the kinds of insights and synchronicities that send shivers of enchantment down your spine.

Whenever you feel "shivers."
it means that you've just had a brush with Universal Truth.

The delights of love and knowledge will seem absolutely incredible. Every moment of every day, you'll feel the power of creation running through your body like a current. Swirls of light and color activate of information to your ever-awakening soul. Burdensome and frightening things you thought were "real" in the lower realms are not real. Delicious feelings of contentment, certainty, and peace, beyond all measure, will be yours as you realize fear is an illusion. This realization will be a soothing relief compared to the heavy weight you carried in earlier densities. Whenever you feel a sensation of soothing relief, you're coming into resonance with your higher self.

Reality vs. Illusion

A major milestone of your 5D curriculum will be mastering discernment of what's real and what's unreal. The fifth chakra teaches us about truth versus falsehood. Knowing the difference is called WISDOM.

A Course in Miracles says, "Nothing real can be threatened. Nothing unreal exists. Herein lies the Peace of God."

We could call whatever is unreal an illusion. The word "illusion" can be confusing. An illusion is a false appearance or apparition, and therefore it cannot be ultimate reality. **Everything which has been created by your mind has lost some of its original perfection along the way.** This means that all the created worlds are in some state of illusion.

Does that mean created things do not exist? They DO exist, but only in your mind or perception. **Creation exists in a dream-like state within your mind. You have made it all up!** This may not make sense now, but when you reach 5D, you'll totally get it. Nothing's really here but the Reality of the Source Field.

Quantum physics tells us this is true. Every created thing isn't really a "thing" at all. It's just a thought.

As you become free from your attachments to anything that's "unreal," a deep and everlasting peace will come over you and will be yours to keep. Fifth Density is the station of certainty. It is the station of knowing. It is the station of wisdom. Imagine how much less fear you will have once you really understand what Truth is and what Truth is not. **You'll no longer believe in a world that is made up of projections from your own lower mind. You will believe only in the Truth.** The Truth will set you free (from attachments), and freedom brings with it the Peace of God.

Many people want to stop here in their growth because it feels so amazingly good. But this place is not the end of your journey. At a certain point, you find that even the gorgeous kaleidoscopic-reality of Fifth Density won't take you all the way to complete remembrance of Who You Are. You must continue your evolution toward the level of the Spirit in 6D.

Summing up the Fifth Soul Level

Fifth Density is one in which every citizen is pure of heart and impeccably responsible for the highest good of ALL. Being given the honor of possessing immensely powerful skills such as conscious manifestation, which is the ability to manipulate time and space, requires tremendous self-integrity. It takes a huge amount of refinement to be ready to use these remarkable abilities. Fifth Density is an effortless society where everyone's contributions collectively come together to produce lives of joy and bliss for all.

Your Last Task in 5D

You, as Celestia, have attained much by now. You've got a good start on your journey through the "Worlds of Light" as you've left the physical worlds behind. You're beginning to remember the Truth of Who You Are. But you still have a way to go. While Fifth Density is beautiful and etheric, you still possess a subtle, separate self which sees itself as unique from others and separate from God. These limitations hold you back from experiencing the deep, hidden Truths that you'll find in Sixth Density.

The last task of Fifth Density is to let go of the final wisps of **the glamour mystical powers.** Superpowers such as telepathy, knowing the future, and telekinesis are glamorous and fantastical! But beware – feelings of wonder and awe at the mystical delights of 5D are not the ultimate attainment. **You must give up any attachment to the distortions of multidimensional ability.** There is more beyond this.

The principle 5D task requires that you surrender to light/love completely. You will have to make a choice to stop looking at anything else, including the ability to manifest, mysticism, magic, ESP, or personal superpowers. You must let these things go. God is your only choice now. The Sufis call this the state of "Fana," (Fa-naa) which means the spiritual act of choosing to tame your own will to follow the highest light you can reach. **When you allow your lower self to dissolve into Light/Love, you leave your ego-trash behind and take on more of the qualities of God-mind.** Only then will you be ready to cross through the vibrational gateway into Sixth Density.

Chapter 11

The Sixth Level of Soul Evolution
Unity

The moment I first heard of love
I gave up my soul, my heart, and my eyes.
I wondered, could it be that
the lover and the beloved are two?
No, they have always been one.
It is I who have been seeing double.
~ Rumi

The Experience of the Sixth Soul Level

Shifting from Fifth Density to Sixth Density means making a qualitative change in your **understanding of multiplicity versus unity.** Sixth Density corresponds to the sixth chakra in the body and the sapphire light ray on the visible spectrum. The action step in this density is **to totally surrender your individuality**. It was impossible, up until crossing the Sixth Density portal, to really know true unity. Even though you probably had fleeting tastes of unity through peak states, you could not fathom 6D before. This place is ULTRA advanced!

At this soul level, all knowledge gets pooled among individuals so that a collective consciousness runs everything. When you graduate from a 5D light-body to a 6D collective consciousness, you'll keep the knowledge from everything you ever learned: primal existence (1D), instinct and emotion (2D), personal power, (3D), compassion (4D), and wisdom (5D), but a new component will be added into the mix: **the experience of ONENESS. You will BE your neighbor. And he will BE you.**

This is the first time in all of evolution that you'll experience Love as TOTAL – for the self, for the other, and for all things everywhere. Everyone is known to be One Being. Trust between beings is absolute. For the first time, even the slightest drop of negative polarization is unable to exist. This realm is totally good and totally light. Not even a teeny thought which is out of alignment with Truth could be tolerated by the vibration of Light and Truth that makes up this world. You could say that the light would "burn" it. In this way, light purifies confusion into right alignment. Light disintegrates anything unlike itself. You may have experienced some "peak states" of this reality before now, but you won't be able to hold them until you transition through the 6D gate.

For the first time in all of your created existence, **the "many" will be experienced for what it is – a delusion.** *There never were many.* There was only One. A lot of 3Ders know about unity <u>intellectually</u>, but possessing 6D consciousness is a whole different experience. This is complete immersion. It's a full-on experience of the entire cosmos as one great movement. You couldn't see it before because of the design. It was necessary for you to experience "others" outside yourself. You had to learn all about your unique, individual facet of self, first. Seeing life from separate points of view wasn't BAD or WRONG. It's what you were supposed to be doing! God desires for us to experience EACH ONE of those points of view in order to weave the entire tapestry properly. God needed you to try on multiple points of view, because, remember, HE wanted to see them thorough your camera lens.

Through the process of moving through the densities on your Soul Map, each seemingly individual soul will eventually integrate together. All people will join. You will LOVE IT this way! No one feels resistance at the Sixth Density level because assimilation into the Godhead is blissful. In 6D – all individual points of view will collapse into a singularity which you will experience as UNION.

Nothing will seem remotely meaningful from before. You just won't care about the old stories and dramas. Bliss and peace are the only real things. You will know that Love is all there ever was, and those stories were just hallucinations you made up. **You will know that you are not only *PART* of All-That-Is, but that you *ARE* All-That-Is.** Everything that came before will seem to you like a dream.

Encoded in your sixth chakra are the tools you need to learn about the following attributes:

• Coming to understand the real meaning of unity,

- Living in absolute whole-ism,
- Experiencing everyday activities as holy, sacred and Joyous,
- Experiencing every moment as bliss,
- Experiencing relationships as a means to merge and unify,
- Fireworks are felt every moment (not just in the "good times," but all the time) because every connection ignites the full flowering of your soul.

The Sixth Density Kit

When you incarnate into any density, you receive a body/mind which outfits you with everything you need to get along in that realm.

Your Light Body Kit

Sixth Density is another World of Light, but it contains even more light than the other densities. This light isn't like 3D Earth light. It's more pure than the sun. It has no heat. It has no color. Light isn't a feeling or a thing - so what is it? **Light is an amalgamation of information mixed with active loving.** It is a dynamic, animated light, which has the power to create.

Physical matter will no longer exist like the kind 3Ders are used to. Even the "plasma-like" matter of 5D has been purified into pure light. Your body will be pure light – similar to the one you had in 5D, only even less materialized. Your body will be made of super-charged information/love. It will be vastly upgraded to allow you to experience even more complex, multi-dimensional thought. Your body will run incredible amounts of wattage through it. Its energy circuits will have to be powerful enough to handle unimaginable volumes of information.

Your body won't have the same human-shaped form you've been used to, because your soul will have expanded like the vast horizon at sunrise. Now, all beings are seen as only one being, one body; and the body is like nothing you can presently imagine. If you wish to take "human" form, you will be able to, but most of the time you won't want to. It's hard work for 6Ders to downgrade their vibration so much as to take on Third Density form. Plus, being vast is a lot more fun!

Unity is a spiritual state in which all souls are joined as one. To grasp this concept, let go of the idea of individuality and try to sink into imagining a heavenly realm where every soul still possesses his own facet of the Divine, but he no longer lives from it. He is no longer defined by his individuality. He no longer cares about being separate because this new kind of harmony feels so good. Everyone will live and work as One Seamless Consciousness. Effortlessly, this One Being will move about its learning. In 6D, there will neither be any physical world, nor any physical bodies to take care of. Instead of using so much energy to survive (like you do in 3D), you will use 100% of your energy to love and grow.

**The entire created Universe itself
is made up of consciousness bound by Love.
True wisdom guides all things.**

In 6D, you'll be able to know each person, place and thing in every density, in its totality. You will know everyone. Everything in creation exudes a subtle soul-signature in ways you can't sense yet on 3D Earth. Imagine a place where the colors are luminous, and even more than that, the colors are LIVING aspects of being!

In 6D, all of the mystical realities of creation are revealed. You'll develop maximal sensing power – much more than your five

physical senses could ever detect or understand. Everything you see will instantaneously reveal its true soul-nature to you.

Think of the way a flower emanates a fragrance. Back in 3D, you experienced that fragrance as a smell. You breathed it in through your nose and your brain translated that information as a pleasant aroma. In Sixth Density, however, that flower's fragrance is experienced one-thousand times more exquisitely. **The fragrance you smell is literally the soul-essence of that flower-being.** When you "breathe in" the soul fragrance of the flower, its aroma is its way of *communicating to you Who It Is*. The flower LOVES when you admire it. You can receive complete information about that one particular flower through a delightful fantasia of your non-physical senses. This is how entirely we can know all other living beings in 6D – **we know them so intimately, we can smell the fragrance of their soul.**

Your Mental Kit

In sixth density, you'll be able to track thoughts (your own, and others') by watching thought-geometry unfold. Thought moves constantly, even in Third Density, but in 6D, you'll experience thought as a colorful medley like an orchestra of thought and senses. Ideas will look like shapes morphing, one into the next. How beautiful it will be to **watch a thought process unfold** like artwork!

When you're incarnated in a sixth density lifetime, all you will have to do is think a thought toward a friend, and she will receive it instantly. She's not separate from you. It's hard to imagine with the 3d brain, but she is both a distinct person, and also she is melded with you.

The truth is: there never was any physical world.

Previously, in 5D, you became a master of creating your world, but in 6D, you won't be creating physical-looking worlds anymore. In truth, there are no bodies or houses like you think of in your present state. 6D souls live in the cosmos, but not even our physical cosmos. They live in a different realm altogether from our "space" which has stars and planets. You perceive your 3D world as "space/time." 6Ders perceive their world as "time/space." In Sixth Density, you'll literally be living in the realm of angels. Your world looks more like colorful swirls where everyone lives in perfect peace. Barely remembering the limitations of separation, you will experience 6D as an overwhelming feeling of closeness to God.

Your Emotional Kit

In 6D, **every single soul becomes, desires, and is willing to give up his individuality to return back to the unity** from which we all began. At this point in your evolution you won't want individuality anymore – so don't worry now that you'll miss it. You will be more than happy to give all that up for the bliss of living in unity.

Even though this realm seems so very heavenly, souls are still learning. These are the Holy Lessons of Light, mostly unfathomable to a 3Der. You, as a 3Der, may be able to reach a peak state in prayer or meditation now and again. Bits of 6D unity may be revealed to you on special occasions, as when you're in the depths of meditation or prayer. You may have had some experience showing you that all of humanity is ONE. By and large, it is very difficult for a 3Der or even a 4Der to understand Unity - much less hold it for any length of time. If you don't understand it, use that knowledge as a sign to help you determine your level. All you need to know is that unity does exist at the higher realms, and that one day, you will live within it.

Becoming Whole

Souls become whole when they decide to stop *resisting what IS*, and stop *desiring what IS NOT*. Peace comes when one accepts that which is real, and disavows that which is not real. Remember what A Course in Miracles says, "Only Love is Real." That kind of rules out *EVERYTHING else but Love*, doesn't it?

Back in 4D, you learned to accept everything as it showed up – whatever it was. Whether it felt good and right, or bad and wrong, it was important to say YES to it. That's acceptance. **Acceptance is to let everything BE OK as it IS.** Saying YES or accepting was a vital process in 4D that gave everything the space it needed to exist, so that it could be properly loved.

In Sixth Density, acceptance takes on a whole different meaning. What you are about to learn may seem paradoxical to what you just read, but try to hear this with a multidimensional mind. In 6D, souls can only experience that which resonates with the highest self. Souls in Sixth Density do not accept any false idea, illusion or stray emotion as something Real. A 6Der is capable of seeing and understanding all the levels, but because he knows the follies and foibles of lower realms are not real; he doesn't acquiesce to their reality. This might be considered "rejection", but paradoxically, 6D souls still love and accept everything. They know what's not in alignment with Source exists on other levels, but they dismiss it because they know it's not Real. You could call it *Holy Discernment.*

6D souls want nothing but to be as near as possible to God and to be of service to all inhabitants of the Universe. 6D souls are free and whole.

"The entrance to 6D is
knowing, being, and living
In the space of wholeness."
~ Chris Madsen

An Incarnation in the Sixth Soul Level

You've finally crossed through the portal to 6D. You're emergence does not come about as a result of two beings choosing to give birth to you. You are completely in charge of everything that happens to you. You give birth to yourself. Imagine that a cloud of pure, nebulous consciousness gives birth to something incredibly focused. That's you. Once here, you arrive as a being called Angelo. Angelo spends lots of time getting used to this world. It's like nothing he's experienced before. You as Angelo may arrive on a planet, but maybe not. **If there is a planet, you live *with* the consciousness of the planet-being's energy, and not *on* the planet like a parasite.** Angelo's body is like mist. Every molecule is powerfully conscious. It is Angelo's task here to awaken each molecule of his being. It is his task to master his ability to envelop all of creation. He knows everything about lower physicality and universal energy, and how all the lower worlds are built.

Angelo has an enormous amount of compassion for Earth humans. Together with the rest of his 6D collective of souls, they work to help the beings in the lower realms. Angelo sometimes takes an **energetic human form** (usually not physical) and appears to Third Density people, giving them guidance and support. When you, as Angelo, do visit Earth, 3Ders call you an "angel." What is an angel or spirit guide, but a very highly evolved being who lives very close to God? The angels are people just like you. They are just entities who have journeyed all the way through the densities like you are doing, in order to arrive at a station of unity. To Third Density humans, 6Ders appear as light beings. 6Ders have very few "veils" covering their pure essence because they have walked through, and experienced all the levels of the Soul Map.

Society in the Sixth Soul Level

In Sixth Density, the social arena will be unlike that which you experienced in 3D. You'll no longer engage in politics, organizations, clubs, task groups, etc. Even families are unnecessary, because everyone is one big family. All people live as One Mind, contributing his or her individual knowledge and experience to the Whole as needed.

Think of a bee hive. Each bee knows what her personal job is, and yet, she lives for the safety and good of the whole community. Bees have been known to commit suicide en masse to protect the others during floods or freezes. Their society is called the "hive mind." This is a bit like the way a collective-level of existence feels. No one is sad that they aren't "special." **The need for special love has been transcended.** Each individual spark of God is happy to be what it is, a soul integrated into the whole with everyone else.

Love Relationships in the Sixth Soul Level

In Angelo's distant past, he used to form romantic bonds with others for the sake of "special love." Instead, in 6D, he feels expanded love for all beings. Angelo is in love with everyone and everyone is in love with him. The highest, most idyllic, fleeting love-state that he ever felt back in 3D is his constant feeling-state all the time now in Sixth Density. You, as Angelo, love all the worlds, all the beings, yourself, and God, with total, never-ending devotion. You even love the negatively-polarized beings (the bad guys) because you have completely understood the secret of forgiveness. You are in a continual state of ecstasy, much like that which your religious texts speak of when they describe heavenly realms. This IS the heavenly angelic realm.

Sex is a thing of the past, since there are no bodies. Even the merging you experienced in 5D isn't necessary, since Unity is an experience which FAR exceeds the pleasure of merging. You, as Angelo, don't miss physical sex in your life in Sixth Density. The experience of Oneness is profoundly intoxicating and perennially captivating. *Physical sex is a very poor substitute.* Looking back, 3D sex will seem like a pale, clumsy, rudimentary way of connecting.

Time in the Sixth Soul Level

Since time becomes irrelevant in 6D, you'll be able to go backward and forward in time at will. You'll also be able to live within timelessness, if you choose. You'll see all the parallel realities, all the timelines that ever happened or ever will happen. You'll visit them and assist as often as possible.

Imagine saying your prayers before bedtime. What if **the angel you pray to before you go to bed is YOUR OWN 6D SELF, traveling backwards in time to help you?** Since there is no time, your higher self can visit you at any time. Your 6D self can don any costume when he comes to you, such as a physical, etheric, light body, symbol, dream, or vision costume. Your future self as Angelo only wants one thing for the 3D you. His sole purpose is to help you understand how to break through the limitations of your own belief systems.

Have you ever seen or sensed an angel or spirit guide? These beings are merely evolved humans. Have you ever encountered a peaceful non-terrestrial? The peaceful ones are likely 5D or 6D people. They may be people from other places in the galaxy, but they're still *people* with lives, relationships, children, loves, and dreams. They aren't so different from us. They have a chakra system. They have an emotional GPS system. They possess an internal Soul Map. They have evolved from First Density all the way through every density - just like Earth humans do. Higher non-terrestrials have spiritual lives and seek to remember their soul origins, just as you do. Positive higher ETs are very quiet. 5D and 6D people are completely beyond living in a flashy way. They are internally focused on God, the Source of All-That-Is, and are intensely set on their own evolution/learning, and on assisting all created beings with their process of shedding any ideas based on ir-reality.

Spirituality and Religion in the Sixth Soul Level

Creation started with God's thought. Then God gifted us free-will to be, do, and create anything we wanted to. God gave souls the freedom to choose darkness or light. He gave us the freedom to hurt people or care for people. God allowed everything. God created us so we could learn step after step, that we, too, are Creators. God gave us the freedom to explore ourselves from bottom to top in order to remember Who We Really Are.

A Course in Miracles says, **"All minds are joined."** This is a 6D Truth. We can begin to learn this truth while we're still in 3D, but it won't be fully rooted in our being until 6D consciousness is achieved.

Any religious dogma went out with Fourth Density. Now, 6D, there are no vestiges of it left at all. Religion, itself, is a Third Density feeble attempt to try to understand who God is, and how one fits in the universe.

Sixth Density beings are the people who are visiting humans and giving them the Truths upon which those religions of old are based. Jesus was a highly developed soul. Buddha was a highly developed soul. Moses, Mohammad, Vishnu, Shiva, Quetzalcoatl... they were all higher density souls who visited, or incarnated on Earth to help. Many pure-hearted people have been visited by 6D beings, and have gone on to write beautiful stories about those visitations. Many of the books of the Bible, and other sacred texts, were written by people who were given inspirational Truths by higher density beings. Mohammad was given the Qur'an by an "angel." Joseph Smith founded Mormonism after being visited by an "angel." **It's all just people teaching people**: higher density beings passing down their wisdom to lower density beings. This is how evolution has worked since the beginning of time.

Spirituality in Sixth Density cannot be separated from God. Spirituality no longer encompasses studies of Eastern practices, yoga, meditation, prayer, mindfulness or the like. All of those practices were only tools to help you connect with your higher self when you were a younger soul.

Remember Spot, the Second Density dog? Spot looked up to his master like she was God. As a person travels up the levels, he stops making "idols," or what could be called "illusionary placeholders" in lieu of God.

In 3D, it wasn't always politically correct to talk about God, spirituality, or religion to others. You didn't want to step on anyone's toes or possibly offend. Not so in Sixth Density. There's no beating around the bush talking about God anymore. God is all that is focused on. Nothing else.

Contact

Third Density humans often do have extra-terrestrial or extra-dimensional contact with fourth, fifth, sixth, and seventh Density people. Most don't know how to explain the experiences they have with these higher beings. We give these mystical beings all kinds of names, and we make up stories about what they are and what they can do. Many Third Density humans perceive higher-density beings as "angels," "E.T.s," "extra-dimensionals," "entities," "ghosts," or "Gods and Goddesses." These names are our human attempts to refer to other-worldly beings. Higher-density beings seem very unlike Earth humans because when viewed through our veils, they look like beings of light. Sometimes they appear in a traditional human form, but sometimes they appear in abstract colors and shapes.

In his book, *The Watchers: Lost Secrets of Ascension, Resurrection and Perfection,* William Henry tells us, "During the renaissance, there was a belief developed that the seraphim were actually transformed humans, humans who have transformed themselves into pure light, pure love, and now dwell at God's Throne in Sion. They phase back and forth between the Earthly realm and the heavenly realm, just on the edge of human imagination" (Henry, 2015).

Religious texts are full of stories about "celestial beings." Most of the authors seemed quite awe-stricken when they experienced these beings. For good reason! 6D beings are made of a light so potent and pure, it's simply indescribable. When a higher being's presence is made aware to a lower density being, a whole host of emotions may be felt: fear, confusion, awe, inspiration, bliss...

One thing is for sure — a lower density being doesn't really understand what he is experiencing during or even after these encounters. No one can completely understand 6D until they graduate into it. That's why we find so many myths about the higher realms. These theories aren't altogether accurate, but they are humanity's best attempts at explaining what has been witnessed.

Prayer: Receiving Assistance from Sixth Level Beings

3Ders don't really understand what they are doing when they pray. In truth, the act of prayer is a communication with high-density beings. Many people pray directly to God. God does hear our prayers, but if we remember the way He set up creation, we realize that God doesn't respond directly to our requests. He gives that job to the Sixth and Seventh Density folks. It is Angelo's job to interface with the people of the lower densities. **Remember — God created us, then we, as a collective consciousness created our worlds.** God is the great Architect. The great Overseer. But God does not intervene with your experiences on your journey through the Soul Map. Angelo, Celestia, and other beings are responsible for helping, providing assistance, and teaching lower worldly inhabitants. **This doesn't mean that God doesn't exchange LOVE with you!** HE DOES.

PRAY CEASLESSLY TO LOVE GOD
and to remember the TRUTH of yourself!

For 6Ders, there is an overwhelming sense of wanting to help the lower worlds. Angelo and his friends have learned so much. They want to pass it on. The yearning to help, to teach and to give reassurance is very strong. However, it's not as easy as it may seem. The first cosmic law of the Universe is free-will.

177

Higher-realm beings can only intercede if they are *invited*. This is why asking for help is so important.

Some 3Ders wonder why the angels and multidimensional beings don't just land their ships on the White House lawn and announce their presence. Wouldn't it be reassuring to know they exist and are helping us? Celestia of 5D and Angelo of 6D would love to be invited to visit Earth in physical or etheric form and impart their wisdom. But they are barred. Their hands are tied. Why? **Because so many Earth humans aren't ready to see them.** 5Ders and 6Ders are required to follow cosmic law. They are bound to uphold the law of free-will. If there are humans on Earth who aren't ready, the multi-dimensionals cannot come because it would violate the free-will of those who do not want to know. So they wait. Instead, they communicate to individuals through dreams, visions, synchronicities, mental interference, books, lectures, podcasts, and sometimes direct, personal meetings.

It's frustrating for those who long for contact. So many awakening 3Ders and empaths are ready for change. So many 3Ders are ready to shift to Fourth Density! And think of the lonely Fourth, Fifth, and Sixth Density Volunteer Souls who currently inhabit human form on Earth right now. It's excruciating for them to wait. (Much more will be discussed about "Volunteer Souls" in Chapter 13.) But wait they must - until a majority of humans are ready to face the truth. Even more frightening to the average Joe is the idea of facing the lies which he has been told all his life by his governments and religions. Most 3Ders would prefer to stick their heads in the sand. That's ok. We can love them anyway. We can wait with patience for The Great Awakening that we know will inevitably come.

Veils of the Sixth Soul Level

It may seem like there are no limitations in Sixth Density at all, but actually there are. 6Ders are still learning the ropes of unity throughout their time in this density. They've only just become celestial beings and still have much to learn before graduating into Seventh Density.

There is only one limitation in all of creation, and that is: you are not the Original Source. The Creator created you, not the other way around. God gave you free-will to do anything you want EXCEPT be the Source. So, essentially, you are allowed to do anything you want within the created worlds. You're allowed to go as slow as you want. You're allowed to resist the inevitable evolutionary changes you're heading for. You're allowed to believe in God or not. Just because you choose not to believe in something, doesn't make it untrue. **Learning that you have (nearly) unlimited power within the creation is the reason the seven density curriculums were made.**

The Last Tasks of the Sixth Soul Level

Before you attain the resonance required to pass through the gateway to 7D, you must finish your last tasks. **You must surrender your strong desire to help. You must surrender the part of you that identifies with, and enjoys being part of a collective. You must surrender your attachment to everything that is not God.** It's hard to fathom what this means now. It seems mystifying, but it takes a long time and a lot of intricate learning to master all of that. When you arrive at the gateway, you will know what you need to do.

Perfect trust in the Universal Plan is the resonance one must attain in order to pass through the 7D gateway. Perfect peace is achieved when the attachments of the lower worlds have been completely released.

Chapter 12

The Seventh Level of Soul Evolution

The Doorway to Eternity

"In time, we exist for, and with, each other.
In timelessness, we CO-EXIST with God."
~ A Course in Miracles

In your true home, which you never left, where you are still living with God even now, you need nothing because *you have everything*. Of course, when you're an inhabitant of Third Density, all of that has been forgotten. The holy design made you forget. You were meant to believe in the created worlds that you traveled through. They were meant to seem real to you. It was part of the Divine plan, serving both you and God.

**In traveling through The Soul Map,
God was able to observe and love Himself in the second person.**

Seventh Density is very, very close to the original Homeland. If a need arises in Seventh Density, it will automatically be provided to you. Certainty, all-pervading-peace, silence of mind, and everlasting love are the overall feelings, because once you reach this level, you will know who you are, and you will know who your Creator is.

Seventh Density corresponds to the crown chakra of the energy body, and the violet light ray on the visible spectrum.

When you graduate from a 6D unified energy body to a 7D *cosmic* body, your unity nature will remain, but a new component will be added into the mix: you'll know the BIG PICTURE. **The action step in this density is *reuniting back home with God*.**

In this level you will know what all of creation is, and what it <u>never was,</u> but only appeared to be. You will know that all of the created worlds – even the Worlds of Light - were just grand illusions for the purpose of your own unfoldment. You will understand what all the pain was for. You will understand what all the drama was for. You will know everything.

The 7D Kit

The Physical Aspect of Seventh Density

In Seventh Density, you won't have a physical body. Just like in 6D, your being will be unimaginably vast as you will continue to fuse with All-That-Is. Seventh Density is very difficult to describe with words at all, because living there is like living on the breath of God.

Seventh Density beings are often called "The Guardians" by mystics and seers. If they choose to incarnate, Seventh Density beings can become planets, stars, nebulae, or other galactic beings. They are capable of taking physical form in order to descend down into the lower worlds for contact, but usually they do not. They leave the job of human interfacing to the 5Ders and 6Ders.

The Emotional Aspect of the Seventh Soul Level

Emotions as you know them in Third Density have long been overcome. 7D beings feel love in more varied ways than all the grains of sand on Earth. Love is the essence of everything, and 7D beings see only Love. Living in 7D is like living inside a web of Divine Love.

The Mental Aspect of the Seventh Soul Level

7D beings are what many might call "Arch Angels." When you reach Seventh Density, you will become aware of everything in all of the created worlds because you will have lived them all. Everything that you know is completely unfathomable to 3Ders. 7D is in every way – "heavenly." Reason is no longer needed because it has been replaced by ETERNAL KNOWING. Hence, there is mental silence and complete clarity. A better word for knowing might be "GNOSIS." The old ways of mentalizing, intellectualizing and logic are completely unnecessary because everything is intimately integrated into the ALL.

The consciousness of Seventh Density beings is collective. It's a bit like birds that fly in unison without shouting directions at each other. The birds just KNOW. 7Ders just know. You will know what everyone is thinking, feeling, and doing at all times. You will intimately know every being in your domain. Trust is absolute. No one breaks the rules in Seventh Density. The souls who reside in this level are impeccably learned and cannot think outside of light and wholeness. These beings oversee the whole seven-density-system! That's right, they are the real Guardians of the Galaxy!

An Incarnation in the Seventh Soul Level

Your name is Andromeda. A soul cannot be born into Seventh Density. You *emerged* through the gateway. Your incarnation is simply to exist, immersed in All-That-Is, and immersed in nothingness simultaneously. There are no parents, and you have no body to give birth to. There is no gender in 7D. You are etheric essence without polarity. One lifetime may last a billion years. You are as vast as the space between stars. Since there is no way to measure things in Seventh Density, it's hard to describe your size. You, as Andromeda, hold so much information within your being, that if a 3Der lay his eyes upon you for one moment in your natural state, it would annihilate his station of being. Your light would blind eyes made of flesh and blood. Andromeda's beauty comes from her total synthesis with all creation which comes from her flawless Love and her immaculate, blemish-free soul. You, as Andromeda are aware of every person who has never conceived of a being like you. They may not know you, but you know them. You are one with them.

You as Andromeda are still learning. It might be more accurate to call it *remembering* the tiny shards of amnesia that still exist from so very long ago when you first started your journey through the created worlds. You are built to operate on a cosmic scale. You are made to process so much information at once that a physical body would never be able to handle all your wattage. You are made of pure consciousness - the Source Field itself. You are made of something totally inexpressible. Something totally undefinable. You are made of the energy that creates universes. **In fact, you are the one who CREATED the solar systems and galaxies you have inhabited**. All of that time, you just didn't know how it worked yet. Now you know. It's your job to watch over all the beings who live within your domain. What you're learning is the *all-ness* of everything, and the *non-existence* of everything. **You're learning that everything is, and is not.** You as Andromeda have given up her interest in drama of any kind. You live as a pure co-Creator with God.

Time in the Seventh Soul Level

Remember back in previous chapters when we discussed Einstein's theory of relativity? We talked about the consequences of consciousness catching up with the speed of light. The closer one's consciousness gets to the speed of light, the more time seems to slow down when compared to everything else. In 7D, your frequency will surpass the speed of light, many times over. TIME WILL SEEM INFINITE TO YOU. **That means that your experience of time will be that there is no time.** You'll be able to make a moment last forever, or you could make it last a second. You'll be able to move forward or backward in timelines. The universe will be yours to travel in any direction, and in any density or dimension you like. In this strange domain where time is infinite, you'll experience it as a place of celestial, swirling lights with boundless potentialities. You will have the ability to do what you wish, when you wish. There is one limitation – and that is that you may only do what is in alignment with The All Knowing Source Itself.

7Ders can enter time if they wish, but rarely do so. When you reach this place, you will live in a world of Holy Beingness all the time. You'll be so close to returning back to the heart of God, the place we all came from, that the 7D experience will feel like a wispy dream. *A Great Paradox.* There is creation and non-creation at the same time. You'll have one foot in the world of creation, and one foot in the world of Eternity. 3Ders on planet Earth will perceive you as an angel, **or often mistake you for God,** for they won't be capable of understanding what you are.

From the vantage point of 7D, you'll be able to see that time is not uni-directional, nor is it static. You'll know that time is a construct of consciousness, and only an illusion. When you do look into space/time, what you'll see is a multitude of fluid lines, crossing and intersecting each other. You'll see time as multi-layered. Your mind will be able to hold all of it at once without becoming overwhelmed or confused. **You'll know that time is just a structure within a simulated game** - a matrix made from pure consciousness. The big picture will finally make sense.

While, souls in 7D know that all the densities are happening at one time, time doesn't exist the way 3Ders think it does. **Everything actually happens in chorus, concurrently.** Time only appears to 3Ders as happening in a linear fashion because we are caught in a timeline. There are endless numbers of timelines. You are inhabiting one timeline right now as you read this book.

This is by design for the purpose of your learning, and is actually a gift of mercy for you as you navigate through the lower worlds. In the lower worlds, living in one place at a time, and one moment at a time, allows you to telescope your consciousness down so you can focus on micro-moments. In the lower worlds, God wants you to study micro-moments, because He wants you to get involved as dramas as they unfold, and to learn in sequential order. In the lower realms, you need the perception of time because you're not yet ready to see everything all at once. In Seventh Density, you will be ready. And it will be GLORIOUS!

Helping Lower Density Humans

You, in your incarnation as Andromeda, want to help humans. But let's not forget about the law of free-will, which means you can only assist humans IF THEY ASK. If they don't call out to you, asking for your help, you're not allowed to step in. When humans DO call out for help, they often mistakenly believe you'll save them. **7Ders aren't allowed do for humans what humans won't do for themselves.** Everyone is in charge of their own ascension. It's not Andromeda's job to get involved with petty 3D drama or ego-stories.

This may be the reason so many humans feel as though their prayers aren't answered. You, as Andromeda, ARE answering their prayers. But you're answering them at a level they may not be ready to understand. **7D beings are so highly evolved, they don't even give a second glance to puny ego preferences.** They know that humans believe their problems are huge and important, **but to 7Ders, they are seen as make-believe stories.** These stories are completely unreal. You, as Andromeda, accept the choices lower density beings make and the lives they have chosen to live. However, she sees WAY beyond the small ego. She sees way beyond the heart. She sees way beyond even the supposed spiritual knowledges of ancient cultures. She sees behind all illusions and dreams. She sees only the REAL TRUTH of ALL THAT IS.

Seventh Density holds the Secret of Secrets.
When you arrive in 7D, you, too, will know these secrets.

The Doorway to Eternity

Seventh Density is where the Masters live. When you reach this place, you will sit on high councils that oversee whole solar systems, stars, planets like Earth. You will be one of the Great Ones that 3Ders sense in their dreams and meditations. You will be bound by the moral Truths of God, and you will not break them.

Your Last Task in the Seventh Soul Level

Seventh Density is the doorway to forever. After 7D is transcended, your soul will completely merge back into the Godhead, where it started from. **The final act of mastery in 7D is to remember, for certain, that you ACTUALLY NEVER LEFT HOME,** just like Dorothy in the Wizard of Oz.

The greatest secret in all creation is that <u>the created worlds never were.</u> One day, you will wake up from this dream and realize that every lifetime was just a *thought in the mind of The First Created Being of Light.* None of it actually happened; you only believed that it did. When you realize this with all of your being, and you let go of all attachments to your beliefs about creation, then you will be ready to graduate from Seventh Density and go back Home. This will be the best day of all your "lives."

Why the heck did you go through all of this, only to return home to realize it was all a dream? What was the point? Well... you did it for God. Every sacred text says that the Creator had a passionate wish to perceive Himself in the second person. You agreed to give yourself to that task out of infinite Love for your Creator.

**God, in all of his Wisdom, created a
mirror of Himself into which He could gaze.
YOU are that mirror.**

Through gazing into the mirror of His creation, God is experiencing everything about Himself. He is experiencing all the iterations of everything that could ever be. **He is experiencing all that is destined to be revealed and all that is destined to remain hidden**, and He LOVES every aspect. How joyful it must be for God to be able to experience and Love every fragment of Himself that ever could exist!

**All the lives you have lived, and all that you have learned
are your gifts of LOVE to God.**

191

.

Chapter 13

A Distinct Type of Human: The Volunteer Soul

Cosmic Helpers

*"A higher-dimensional ET soul incarnates
in the normal way (as a baby),
to aid the evolution of humanity and the planet.
This process of cosmic soul-wandering has occurred since the
beginning of human experience on Earth
and is common throughout the Universe.
It expresses the basic Law of Service
in which elder souls freely go to serve worlds in need."*
~ Scott Mandelker, PhD

It's probably pretty obvious at this point, that I believe the majority of humans on planet Earth are living at the third level of soul evolution. It's also probably pretty obvious that I believe that many people were born at a 3D level of awareness, but are currently evolving into a FOURTH DENSITY STATE IN THIS LIFETIME. These transforming Earth natives are called Empaths. (As this chapter goes on, you'll learn that Empaths are different than Volunteer souls.)

However, you may have a hunch that you (or someone you know) were born with an even higher level of consciousness than most folks. In fact, there are *many* people who are born possessing much higher levels of consciousness. In most cases, these souls came to Earth as visitors, having already lived a significant number of their lifetimes in Fourth Density, Fifth Density, or Sixth Density worlds. Volunteer Souls elect to visit here in this Third Density realm for a reason. What might that reason be?

Why, to HELP Earth ascend, of course!

While you were reading the descriptions of each of the densities, if you recognized yourself as having **capabilities of a higher density _since birth_,** then you are probably a VOLUNTEER soul.

A Call was Sent Out

When a planet is readying itself to make a density shift, a galactic call goes out to beings all over space and time who may wish to come and help. When our volunteers heard the call, they'd been busy living their own higher density lives (4D, 5D, 6D) in their own home worlds. They were learning lessons, growing, and becoming closer to God. They were living full lives. They had friends and relationships with loved ones on their home planets.

When the call went out, these people of higher levels chose to enlist. It's a big sacrifice to come to a largely violent, unpredictable, adolescent planet like Earth. It's an experience that offers big learning opportunities to old souls who want to join up and help.

For those who come to assist, the choice is a no-brainer. There is no hesitation. They don't consider how hard it may be. The drive that brings them here is a deep desire to serve their brothers and sisters from a place of unconditional love. The difficulty of the job only hits them once they've been living on planet Earth for a while. Being human is really hard. It's hard for 3Ders, and it's hard for Volunteers.

Volunteers have been visiting planet Earth in small numbers for eons (think Moses, Da Vinci, Joan of Arc, Emerson, Beethoven, Einstein, Gandhi, Nikola Tesla and so many other brilliant minds from history). It is only in the last 100 years or so that we've had uncommonly large numbers of higher-consciousness-beings incarnating here on Earth. They are coming en masse now, because they want to be of service, and to witness the big show.

An Incarnation as a Volunteer Soul

You, as Willow, are hanging out in your 4D world, swinging on your floating porch swing. You are busy blowing bubbles, and then using your powers of manifestation to turn them into Reese's Pieces, for fun. You, as Willow, receive a scroll requesting all able-bodied fourth, fifth and sixth Density beings to heed Earth's desperate call to usher in the Fourth Density.

Willow unhesitatingly jumps up and makes her way to the nearest inter-density travel agency. She receives her itinerary which instructs her how to transport to Earth. She travels from stargate to stargate, density to density, planet to planet, until she arrives at Earth's astral plane. From Earth's astral plane, Willow is able to enter into the body of a human baby to be born on Earth. Her mission is to help with Earth's ascension process.

Volunteers Aren't Perfect

Volunteer Souls come from elsewhere. They "grew-up" learning their spiritual curriculum on other worlds, in other solar systems, in other galaxies, and in other planes of existence. They lived through First, Second and Third Densities, just like you – they just did it someplace else.

Just because a volunteer is higher-density-activated since birth, does not mean they are perfect. It just means they understand the laws of love because they've already mastered them. They don't buy into Third Density bull because they're so over it. Think of volunteers as just a step or two more experienced than you, and learn what you can from them. These people still have lots to learn, just like you. Its one reason they are here: to learn the lessons of being a volunteer in an alien world. Volunteers are living human lives with higher consciousness minds inside. Because they've incarnated into regular human bodies like yours, they still have human experiences like pain, fear and trauma. They have problems. The DIFFERENCE is that they have a "wiser than their years" vibe. You may get the sense that they know something you don't. Some of them may seem wayyyyy out there. They seem that way because they're not from here, and they don't recognize human customs. Forgive your Volunteer Soul friends for their imperfections and thank them for their service.

Do 7Ders come as Volunteers? Not Usually. Seventh Density is the gateway to eternity, so it's extremely difficult for 7D souls to incarnate into physical bodies. They help in other ways. Seventh Density souls are in charge of much grander business.

They oversee the entire solar system in every aspect from their posts, high up in the realms of timelessness.

Empaths

Lately, the term "Empath" has become widely used. Empath is a name for 3D Earth natives who are engaging in their awakening process. (An Empath is not a Volunteer soul.) Empathy is a natural symptom that shows up when the heart chakra (4D) begins to activate. The word Empath gives folks the language to talk about what's happening to them as they wake up and change. The idea of being an Empath may give you permission to accept that you could indeed be experiencing life differently than non-awakening 3Ders. Realizing, naming, and accepting your awakening process is vital because once the course begins, life will surely start throwing new and foreign challenges at you. You'll want to be clear about what's happening to you.

The Difference Between Empaths and Volunteers

Empaths are 3D Earth natives that are beginning their 4D awakening. Earth natives are people who went through their lower soul levels here on planet Earth, not elsewhere like Volunteer Souls. Many Earth natives are awakening now.

Volunteers are souls who have already transitioned fully into 4D, 5D, or 6D. They travel to Earth to take on human bodies for the sole purpose of assisting Empaths who are ready to shift into Fourth Density Consciousness.

It's important to be very honest with yourself. Try not to assign yourself a spiritual category where you do not belong. We all yearn to be the best we can be. That desire can sometimes get twisted by the ego and be used to inflate our sense of self. It may be tempting to tell yourself you're a Volunteer when you're not, or to believe you're of a higher spiritual station than you really are. If you do that, you won't do yourself any favors. **Your life will not make *more sense* – it will most certainly become more confusing.** We don't want that to happen to you. **Our goal here is to help you discern *exactly* where you are on your Soul Map so you can make choices that lessen your confusion, loneliness, and pain.** That can only be possible if you can be honest enough with yourself to identify your station accurately.

Life is hard. Just because Volunteers came from a higher density doesn't mean that they don't have to suffer along with everybody else on Earth. Volunteers are born into human bodies, so Willow is living under the veil of amnesia just like other humans. She's forgotten who she really is and where she's from. She's forgotten her mission. This sets Willow up for a host of problems that are unique to Volunteers.

Willow has a broader spiritual understanding than Earth natives do. When she was young she had expectations that everyone's life-view was similar to hers. She spent her life trying to figure out why she was so different. Because others made fun of her and shamed her for being different, she often felt depressed and hopeless. Willow assumes that when she loves a person with her sensitive 4D heart, they will love her back with the same unconditional love. However, Earth natives aren't capable of a full understanding of 4D unconditional love. Because of others' misunderstanding of her innate wisdom and abilities, Willow goes through a series of abusive relationships with selfish 3Ders. Her relationship with her parents causes immense grief, and sets her up for low self-esteem because of the weak connection between them. **Willow spends her life feeling hurt and confused because her 4D needs are not met in a 3D world.** Willow often feels terribly alone on Earth.

Willow feels like a fish flopping around out of water, looking for oxygen. However, for a Volunteer, very little oxygen is available in Third Density! **Willow desperately needs other Volunteers to remind her of her origins.** When she is reminded of "home", Willow feels she can breathe again. Her very life-force depends on remembering the Truth.

All People of Various Levels of Awakening are Equally Valuable

In God's eyes, we are all equal, no matter what our spiritual station. Do you believe God values a giraffe more than a snail? Do you think God values a Volunteer Soul more than an Earth native? There is neither shame nor pride in any station. This isn't a contest to see who's more or less awake. We are all exactly where we're supposed to be for the perfect working of the Universe. This book is teaching you how to make a truthful self-inquiry so that you can really KNOW YOURSELF. If you can identify your spiritual station correctly, you'll begin to better understand everything about your life.

"All of the children of God are special,
and none of the children of God are special."

~ A Course In Miracles

I offer a support group on Facebook. If you feel a resonance with the topic of empaths or volunteers, I invite you to join the group for deep, intimate conversations about mysticism and what it's like to live on Earth with a bit more awareness than some others may have. Search *"Paige Bartholomew's Support Group for Emerging Empaths" on Facebook.*

You may also wish to join The Soul Map Discussion Classes, which will be released in 2021, and thereafter can be accessed on my website. Watch my Facebook page or join my newsletter for announcements.

~ ~ ~

Volunteer Soul Self-Assessment

1) Are you highly sensitive to other people's feelings, whether spoken or unspoken?

2) Do you "pick up," and sometimes "act out" emotions that are not yours?

3) Is your natural instinct to be gentle, kind-hearted, and generous with people even if they're not nice to you?

4) Is it your first instinct to see the good in people, even if others aren't seeing the good in you?

5) Do you have a keen truth-ometer? Are you able to sense when someone is lying, hiding information, or speaking insincerely?

6) Do you feel safer with animals and nature than with people?

7) Do you have a strong impulse to change the world, to break social systems, or to shatter old paradigms?

8) Do you have a robust sense of purpose, but perhaps aren't sure what that purpose is?

9) Are you interested in the healing arts, spirituality, or meditation?

10) When you were a child, did the world seem unfamiliar to you? (Maybe the color of the sky seemed wrong. Maybe plants and animals, air or water seemed strange.)

11) Do sensations in your body feel peculiar to you? (Perhaps the sensation of digestion seems unfamiliar, or maybe you feel heavier in gravity than you think you should?)

12) Have you ever looked in the mirror and not recognized your body or face? (Maybe your eyes are the wrong color. Maybe you have the wrong number of fingers. Maybe body hair feels foreign.) Google Body Dismorphic Disorder for more information.

13) Have you ever had the thought that your blood family isn't your real family? Have you ever felt homesickness, as though you miss your real family, or real home?

14) Did you have an imaginary friend as a child?

15) Do you imagine that you should have a superpower, and do you perhaps grieve the fact that you don't? (Like: flying, telepathy, breathing under water, etc.)

16) Do the cruelty, violence, and emotional heaviness of the world frighten you or affect you negatively?

17) Does watching violent or scary media make you feel dirty, or even violated - enough to change the channel or turn off your electronic device?

18) Do you sense that there may be more going on behind the scenes with your government than you're being told?

19) Have you had dreams, out of body experiences, or meditations of a spiritual nature that felt real, induced deep awe, or engendered profound insight?

20) Do you feel as if the majority of the people you meet are unconscious of spiritual things that are second nature to you?

21) Have you ever seen a UFO, been taken onto a ship, or had a meeting with a positively-polarized, loving, higher vibrational being? This could either happen in the flesh, in a dream, or during meditation. (Negative or frightening encounters are a different phenomenon and should not be counted here.)

22) Are you interested in non-terrestrials, angels, and higher density beings?

23) Have you had suspicions that you are from another place, another planet, or from space?

24) Have you ever looked up at the stars and felt longingly, "I want to go home?"

25) Do you feel as if you don't fit in or belong anywhere?

26) Do you think in multidimensional layers of thought? Do you think in geometrical shapes? Color? Sound?

27) Are you on the "spectrum?"

28) Do you feel an uncommon connection to all beings everywhere, understanding innately that there is only one being – and not many?

29) Do you feel an uncommon connection to Creator Source? Perhaps one that frequently brings you to tears? Do you feel you would give for life for God?

If you answered most of these questions with "YES," then you are likely a Volunteer Soul. If you're hungry to learn more about Volunteer Souls, you'll find my second book to be exclusively about such phenomena. In it, you'll learn how to remember who you really are, and you'll learn to diagnose your density level. We'll discuss the unique and intense struggles Volunteer Souls experience while living here on 3D Earth, which no one seems to talk about. We'll discuss how to deal with Earth natives, what's happening to Earth on an evolutionary level, more about divine cosmology, and so much more.

~ SECTION THREE ~

**Doing the Work it Takes
to Ascend Through the Vibrational Gateway**

Chapter 14

Are You Awakening Into the Fourth Level of the Soul?

How can I tell if I'm really ready?

"Yesterday I was clever,
so I wanted to change the world.
Today I am wise, so I am changing myself."

~ Jellaludin Rumi

Section III of this book will teach you how to shift from 3D to 4D. More information about the higher densities will come in following books. Right now, we all need to focus on the actions we must take, and the changes we must make, in order to step out of the Earth realm, into the wondrous 4D GARDEN!

There are three categories of people living on Earth at this time:

1) **Third Density Earth natives who have no interest in changing,**

2) **Third Density folks who are SO excited to shift to 4D they can hardly wait,**

3) **Volunteers who've come to help the world ascend to the next evolutionary level.**

If you're reading this book, you're most likely in category 2 or 3. In this chapter, we're going to take a close look at category 2: Third Density Earth natives who are ready to shift to Fourth Density.

There is a very special kind of person who is currently going through a very special kind of change. She is a Third Density Earth native who is just about ready to make her shift to Fourth Density (or is already in the process).

Earth natives (as opposed to volunteers) are people who have lived out all of their incarnations on this planet Earth since their birth into First Density creation. Never before has this group of Earthlings experienced what's about to come. They've been anxiously awaiting this time in history. These are the people whose time it is to SHINE!! These are the superstars of the day. Every being from our local star cluster has their eyes on them. It's opening night, a sold-out show, and every seat has the best view in the house.

This is the moment you've been waiting for: your ascension through the Fourth Density gateway, to live in the world of the heart.

"Questioner: 'I am assuming [that] this [Fourth Density] vibration started increasing about between twenty and thirty years ago. Is this correct?'

"Ra: 'I am Ra. The first harbingers of this were approximately forty-five of your years ago.'"

~ The Law of One, Session 44:10

The Author of The Law of One tells us that our Earth started its green light ray activation (Fourth Density activation) 45 years before the writing of The Law of One, in 1981. **According to Ra, Fourth Density energies ignited on Earth around the year 1936.** It is my observation that since that time, we've seen more and more people begin to wake up, faster than ever before.

You, as a person making your shift to empath-hood have distinctive qualities, different from the two other groups mentioned in the list above. The 3Ders will stay put where they are. The volunteers aren't shifting, they are just observing. YOU are the one every higher being came here to watch. They are so delighted with all you've done for yourself, and for humanity. Your accomplishments are extraordinary – and rare. It's not too often that a planet ascends through a density gateway. You're finishing up your work, and you're nearly set. Everyone wants to watch you graduate. You are so beautiful to behold. Your heart is ready to bloom into full flower! You possess all the qualities of primed fourth-chakra-activation, while still living in a human body. It's miraculous!

In our present new-age culture, it has become a common occurrence for people to share when they had their "awakening." They exclaim, "I woke up in 2011 when such-and-such happened to me...." Folks are SO PROUD, and so excited about that moment it all started to change for them! Their declaration is actually really important. It was the moment when the consciousness of their heart was roused into realization. No wonder awakening people are bursting to share it!

At the moment that your heart woke up, you began to see the world through new eyes. You started to think with your intuition rather than leaning so much on your intellect. You may have started reading all kinds of books on healing, consciousness, awakening, manifestation, and the like. You may have felt an opening in your heart and become full of care and concern for other people's pain, for disadvantaged people, abused animals, or the environment. You may have launched your own self-love campaign. You started seeing the world with a new kind of compassion.

Since your awakening, you've been excited about what's coming next. You know *something is happening*, but maybe you haven't been sure about what it is. Hopefully after reading this book, it is becoming clear. You've awakened from your long sleepy dream of Third Density into a massive, immediate, and shocking change where Love becomes your worldview.

It really is the most incredible change.

You are different from those who don't want to shift because they are still choosing to play the 3D game a while longer. They don't understand your new "woo-woo hippie-dippie ways." They may feel uncomfortable with the way your heart has become soft and vulnerable. They may want you back the way you were, like in the "good ole' days." Those days may have been good for them, but your good days are happening NOW! You have even better days to come.

Are You Ready to Shift to Fourth Density?

Here's a short list of questions to help you determine if you are beginning to shift to empath-hood, or 4D consciousness:

1)   *Have you experienced an event in your life; an opening where your interests changed dramatically from limited-paradigm thinking to a more expansive way of seeing yourself and the world?*

2)   *Do you find that you're suddenly interested in things like angels, crystals, the healing arts, health and wellness, the environment, activism, or spirituality?*

3)   *Have you started reading all the self-help and spirituality books you can get your hands on?*

4)   *Do you do your best to stop negative thoughts from running your mind, and to replace them with positive ones?*

5)   *Do you have a deep desire to understand and forgive yourself and others?*

6)   *Do you make the health of the planet equal to your own self-convenience?*

7)   *Do you place the wellbeing of the masses on the same level of importance as your own wellbeing?*

8)   *Do you believe you are positively oriented (as opposed to negatively oriented)?*

9)   Do you place more importance on truth than on comfort?

10)   Do you do your best to listen to the voice of your heart more often than the voice of your ego?

The Law of One suggests that humans only need to be doing these things 51% of the time (James A. McCarty, Don Elkins, 1983). If you are, then you are vibrating at a positively polarized heart level and will be ready when the transition comes. If you are still struggling with some emotional wounds, continue striving to improve. Focus on yourself inwardly not outwardly. Your job in order to shift to Fourth Density is to stop looking outside yourself for proof of higher beings/realms/realities. Stop attempting to gain superpowers like ESP, telepathy, psychic communication, and the like. It will only distract you as these are not the superpowers of your Fourth Density (you're overshooting into 5D skills that you're just not ready for yet). You must focus on what it will take to vibrate the same as the Fourth Density gateway, not beyond it.

Volunteer Souls are Here to Help YOU

You're different from a Volunteer Soul because volunteers are *BORN with a higher density program already running.* *Their higher knowing has been online from the moment they were born into human form.* Some Volunteers are aware of their origins, others are not. Fourth Density Volunteer Souls came from a Fourth Density world. Fifth Density volunteers came from a Fifth Density world, and so on. They aren't native to Earth, like you are. They "grew up" in other places. They came here to help you. You might have met a limited number, but comparatively speaking, there are very few Volunteers living on Earth, somewhere between one and three percent, according to The Law of One Material (James A. McCarty, 1983). Volunteer Souls may incarnate in the form of authors, songwriters, clergy, motivational speakers, therapists, scientists, doctors, online personalities, activists, new-agers, lawyers, transformational thinkers, poets, philosophers, housewives, baristas, etc. You may have a friend in your life who was born fourth-chakra-activated or higher. You're even luckier if you have a parent who is a Volunteer Soul. He or she gave birth to you for the purpose of loving you unconditionally, and helping you navigate through the illusions and confusions of 3D life. Not all kids are so fortunate.

How Might The Ascension Happen?

National Geographic News gives us information from Habibullo Abdussamatov, head of space research at St. Petersburg's Pulkovo Astronomical Observatory in Russia. The scientist said, "The Mars data is evidence that the current global warming on Earth is being caused by changes in the sun. The long-term increase in solar irradiance is heating both Earth and Mars." If global warming is happening on Mars and Earth, clearly the problem isn't caused by emissions from SUVs. It's not just Mars that's heating up. All of the planets have undergone very fast, vivid changes in the last 30 years. **Global warming is a solar system-wide event.**

We now have scientific evidence that our solar system is traveling through an enormous cloud of charged particles in outer space. Astrophysicists like Dr. Priscilla Frisch, of the University of Chicago, tell us that the presence of this cloud is very real. Dr. **Frisch says that the cloud can cause sweeping changes to *all* of the planets AND the sun, not just Earth.** "There would be dramatic effects in the inner solar system," comments Dr. Frisch. We are already seeing intense evidence of those changes throughout our cosmic neighborhood.

New science is showing up with proof that our solar system is warming, not because of humanity's abuse of the environment, but because of the hot, interstellar cloud we're entering. NASA's website published an article in December of 2009 called, *Voyager Makes an Interstellar Discovery.* The article states, "The solar system is passing through an interstellar cloud that physicists say should not exist. In the December 24th issue of *Nature*, a team of scientists reveal how NASA's Voyager spacecraft has solved the mystery. 'Using data from Voyager, we have discovered a strong magnetic field just outside the solar system,' explains lead author Merav Opher, a NASA Heliophysicist, guest investigator from George Mason University.'"

NASA goes on to say in the above mentioned article, "Astronomers call the cloud we're running into now the Local Interstellar Cloud or 'Local Fluff' for short. It's about 30 light years wide and contains a wispy mixture of hydrogen and helium atoms at a temperature of 6000 degrees Celsius. Voyager data show that the Fluff is much more strongly magnetized than anyone had previously suspected - between 4 and 5 microgauss" (Phillips, 2009).

Our solar system is encased in a giant protective bubble called the heliosphere. The heliosphere is produced by the sun, and keeps stellar radiation, dust, and other particles away from the inner solar system. The outer edge of our heliosphere is racing into the Local Fluff now. It appears that the cloud is likely responsible for all the interplanetary climate changes we are seeing.

In the artist's depiction that follows, we see our sun as the white dot in the middle of the picture. The big, outer egg-shape that disappears off to the right is the heliosphere. You can see the white-hot interstellar cloud on the left. The artist also shows us where the spacecrafts Voyager 1 and 2 are located in relation to our solar system out in front of us. Information sent back from both Voyagers has helped scientists to discover the cloud ahead of us in deep space. Our solar system isn't standing still – it's traveling through space at a speed of 12 miles per second, or

45,000 miles per hour. We are hurtling headlong, directly into the cloud of hot, magnetically charged particles.

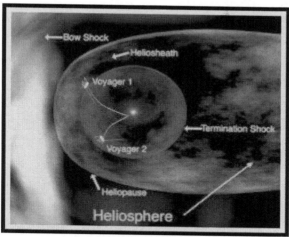

Credit: NASA/Walt Feimer

When we eventually get to the denser parts of the cloud, it has been suggested that the sun could let off a huge burst of energy, dramatically affecting life on Earth as we know it. Some scholars are calling it a "solar flash" or a "solar sneeze." This COULD be the ascension event we've been waiting for.

There is no reason to be afraid of the coming scenario if you raise your vibration to Fourth Density frequency. It's highly probable that the Local Fluff is the gateway to Fourth Density. It's possible that the 6th and 7th density guardians are protecting the solar system until which time the solar system is ascended enough to protect itself.

Whatever means by which ascension will occur for the inhabitants of Earth, one thing is for sure – IT WILL OCCUR. The Divinely designed seven-density model has been in effect since the beginning of time. Beings all over our universe have been growing, learning, and evolving in this manner long before you ever began your enlightenment project in First Density. So, even though we are all feeling impatient, we must trust that the Universe knows what it is doing. Our collective higher selves know how to do this. Your higher self knows how to guide you through these changes.

Chapter 15

Blocks That Keep You From Shifting

Obstructing the Flow of Love
Keeps you Stuck
In the Third Soul Level

"Your task is not to seek for love,
but merely to seek and find
all of the barriers within yourself
that you have built against it."
~ A Course in Miracles

Before we talk about healing and how hugely it affects your shift to Fourth Density, we must take a look at the unhealthy patterns of behavior that humans have used in Third Density for thousands of years. The old ways must be recognized and named before we focus on something brand new.

Remember, Section III is all about learning how to **raise your frequency from third density to fourth density.** We're no longer discussing higher realms, as THIS SHIFT is where our focus needs to be now.

Children's Coping Strategies

When Third Density human beings are very young, their ability to protect themselves from physical, emotional, or psychological danger is limited. Therefore, children will take on any coping responses that seem to help. These strategies DO work, although they're not perfect. They do help soothe a child when adults cannot give them the care that they need. These strategies do help to emotionally whisk a child away, when he or she can't handle feelings that are too big. These strategies are meant to protect the fragile inner self.

3D coping behaviors show up in four main ways: fight, flight, freeze, or fawn.

"Coping Behaviors: The four F's
FIGHT corresponds to narcissism,
FLIGHT corresponds to obsessive/compulsivity,
FREEZE corresponds to dissociation,
FAWN corresponds to codependency."

~ Pete Walker, M.A., MFT

We take our coping behaviors with us from childhood into adulthood. Each of these coping strategies has distinctive characteristics. One of these coping strategies may be used most often, or we may use a combination.

Fight

If your tendency is to go into FIGHT mode when you're feeling threatened, it may look like this: you're cruising along as a child – just being yourself, when a sense of danger shoots through your system. The danger may be real or perceived. It doesn't really matter. You're going to swing into self-protection mode. You may become defensive before anyone says a word. You'll believe you're right and everyone else is wrong. You may become agitated and angry. You'll probably push people away from you, emotionally or physically. **You are a "warrior."** You may blame, and attack, or take away other's rights to have a voice. You may even become aggressive with your words or your body.

These are the maneuvers that protected you best in your family while you were growing up. In a messed-up way, the fight response really did keep you safe. However, it's highly probable that you'll take this response into your adult relationships. **You'll be the partner people are secretly afraid of.** If you don't learn to recognize your 3D patterns of self-protection and replace them with healthier behaviors, you'll create what's called "dysfunctional relationships" that do not work. It's time to simply become mindful of your coping strategies and learn a new way to live.

Flight

If your tendency is to go into FLIGHT mode when you're feeling threatened, it may look like this: as a kid, you're minding your own business just being yourself, when a feeling of threat in the family comes over you. Your sensitivity causes you to shift into self-protection. You may become anxious- even before any outward signs of trouble begin. You can feel it coming. You may even go into a panic. You'll act out by trying to control your surroundings. You may start compulsively picking at your face, or biting your nails. You may start cleaning or washing things, tidying the house. You might start trying to corral your siblings, care-take your mother, or pacify your father. You feel nervous and afraid. You may retreat to your room, but it doesn't stop the anxiety. Hidden away, you feel it more acutely, while obsessive thoughts play over and over in your mind. **You are a "fixer."** You believe that you can fix the problems, if only you had the chance. You may even emotionally blow up, putting the focus on yourself like a sacrificial lamb in an attempt to distract from what's really happening in the house.

These behaviors protected your vulnerable insides when you were a child. However, it's highly likely you'll take these same anxious behaviors into your adult relationships and create dysfunction there. **You'll be the partner who seems overly dramatic.** People may say, "You're too much." They may feel overwhelmed by your emotional reactions. It's time to become aware of the 3D self-protection behaviors you developed in childhood. New healthier behaviors can then be adopted for the sake of your relationships and your own evolution.

Freeze

If your tendency is to go into FREEZE mode when you're feeling threatened, it may look like this: you're poking along, just being a kid, when chaos blows up in the house. Your whole body stops, as if it is paralyzed. Your mind is racing, but your body is frozen. You're terrified. You feel as if you have zero ability to deal with the level of emotion spewing out of everyone around you. You feel inept, incompetent, and hopeless to find a solution. **You're a "hider."** After a few minutes, your mind may go blank, leaving you staring, like a deer in the headlights. People may talk to you, or scream at you, and you just stand there. You may feel nothing. Dissociated. You may end up disappearing from life altogether, burying your tender feelings away because it feels safer that way.

These were the best strategies for you, as a child, to protect your inner vulnerability. However, it's very likely that you'll take these patterns into your adult relationships. **You'll be the partner who "isn't available."** You may believe you're happier on your own rather than in a committed partnership. Distance may make you feel temporarily safe, but it gets in the way of human connection, which you deeply crave and need. It's time to become aware of your 3D dysfunctional coping mechanisms, face your fear, and develop strategies that promote adult intimacy.

Fawn

If you're using FAWN to protect your vulnerable inner parts when feeling threatened, it may look like this: as a child, you're wandering around just being you, when you notice that people around you aren't happy. Adults in your house might be feeling angry, depressed, anxious, or fearful. You want to help. **You are a "server."** You want everyone to be ok. You try to give everyone what they want to make them feel better. When THEY feel better - you feel better. You placate. You people-please. You say yes even when you mean no. Because of that, you may lose your sense of yourself as you blend into everyone else like a chameleon. You might find it hard to know what your own feelings are at any given moment. Because you're not aware of your emotions within, you may look to others to see how they're feeling, in an attempt to make up a fictional set of feelings for yourself. You may worry that you're invisible to others, or it may you that you don't have an identity of your own. You're terrified of anger and conflict, so you'll do anything at your disposal to diffuse the strong emotions of people around you.

For you, FAWNING kept you feeling safe as a child. The problem is that you'll probably take these coping strategies with you into adulthood. You'll be the person who pleases everyone while abandoning yourself. **Because you don't know who you are, you'll be the partner who may "have a mid-life crisis," suddenly changing his mind and even abandoning his commitments mid-stream.** Your sense of self may be frail, therefore creating fragile relationships based on false pretenses. *You may think that making stuff up just to keep the peace is a good thing – but what your partners and friends really need from you is your TRUTH.* You'll only build your own inner strength when you learn to be honest with yourself, and **LIVE that honesty out loud**. This is the inner healing you'll need to be able to evolve.

It Wasn't Your Fault

Often children observe painful adult situations, and then come to the conclusion that the emotional fallout was their fault. Sometimes kids believe that if they were good enough, worthy enough, or strong enough, they would be able to make things happy. **Children cannot *cause* their family's dysfunction, and they cannot *fix* their family's dysfunction.**

We, as parents, must do better. Parenting with an accepting, open heart will give kids a chance to grow up without feeling like they have to protect who they are. It's so important that we grow and change – for ourselves and our children.

Triggers

A trigger is any stimulus that reminds us of a painful moment in our past. A true trigger will take you out of the present moment and throw you into a fight/flight/freeze/fawn state. When you go into one of the "Four F's," your brain literally changes. Your pre-frontal cortex shuts down and your reptilian brain kicks in. It does this automatically without your consent, because the process is an ancient survival mechanism for the human body.

Since a trigger takes you out of your normal sense of reality, it can be called a PTSD (Post Traumatic Stress Disorder) event.

The Three Places from which Triggers Originate

Inter-relational triggers happen between you and another person. These are triggers that happen when another person says or does something that reminds you of a painful past situation when you didn't feel safe. Once you're triggered, it may be hard to stay present.

Internal triggers happen within your own body, mind, or emotional system. Humans store traumatic memories in their bodies. **A physical pain, ache, or illness you're suffering from may actually be caused by traumatic memory**. You may not be aware that the trauma is being held in your body. You may not realize that your illness is in reality emotional pain being expressed throughout your body.

External triggers happen outside your mind or body. These triggers elicit unsafe feelings. Such an event may be an upsetting situation you hear about, like a poor country where the people are starving. It may be a societal issue like the Corona Virus pandemic. It might be a scene in a movie where you see others being hurt or victimized. These scenarios "trigger" your own memories of being hurt or victimized. Once you're triggered, part of you goes into a trance around the pain. Your pain is no longer living in the past. You're feeling it RIGHT HERE, RIGHT NOW.

People usually get triggered so fast they don't realize they're not in their right mind until someone points it out, or until later introspection. **A trigger is a PTSD flashback.** The trauma in your past experience may have been overt, or covert. You may define it as a problem, or you may not. However, if you felt anything in that past experience but support and acceptance, it probably caused stress, which can easily be laid down as a traumatic memory in the brain. You may experience triggers even when you believe you have no trauma in your past. Being a human on planet Earth, "The PTSD Planet," means that triggers are going to present themselves fairly often in your life.

Stay Mindful During a Trigger

All beings protect themselves from discomfort. It's natural. You can't STOP the reptilian brain from getting triggered. You CAN learn to stay awake during a trigger, and realize you have a choice about your next move. You don't have to perpetuate old patterns of dysfunctional, hurtful behavior. As an awakening human, you can learn to override your reptilian brain's coping strategies. You want to make different choices about how you behave when triggers arise. You can teach yourself how to respond and not to react. You want to learn healthy communication skills when you are triggered instead of flying into fight, flight, freeze or fawn. I recommend the book *Non-Violent Communication,* as the book to start with (Rosenberg, 2015). It teaches you to slow down when you're in defense mode so you can learn how to communicate more safely with your partner or friend about what's happening.

Non-violent communication is a 4D skill. Learning to use it means you've succeeded in transforming a part of your brain from the old 3D paradigm, and trained it to think more multi-dimensionally. Identifying your triggers and knowing how to discuss them without defending or attacking is a life-changing skill. It will affect all of your relationships, including your relationships to yourself. Welcome to Fourth Density!

Projection

Carl Jung once said, "A man who is unconscious of himself acts in a blind, instinctive way. He is, in addition, fooled by all the illusions that arise when he sees everything that he is not conscious of in himself, coming to meet him from outside as projections upon his neighbor" (Jung, 1967).

What is projection and how is it used it to attempt to keep ourselves safe?

Let's make this simple. Because you're not perfectly healed yet, your subconscious holds delusional beliefs. For example, you may have a skewed belief that says, "I'm not worth people's time and effort. Men (or women) aren't attracted to me. No one respects my schedule. No one would want to be with me." When a situation comes up in your life similar to those above, that situation will *trigger* those delusional beliefs, making you experience them all over again, in real time.

For example, let's say you are stood up for a date. **The missed date was created by your inner Soul Map to show you where you are believing an old delusion or an emotional distortion that needs healing, such as that which was explained in the previous paragraph.** Being stood up was the situation you created for yourself to give you the opportunity to become aware of the need to heal.

The Sufis say, "Everything is from God, to God." Looked at through a slightly more simplified lens, it can mean, "Everything is from you, for you." **If you could remember that every scenario in your life is pointing directly to the place you need healing, you would have healed yourself long ago!** The best case scenario would be that you apply all meaning to yourself instead of looking to find someone else to blame for your discomfort.

Your persistent, long-standing beliefs (not your fleeting thoughts) are being played out on the stage of your life. The Universe is efficient. **Every situation you find yourself in is perfectly created for your learning.**

**The entirety of your world is a projection.
Like a film projector pointed at a screen,
you're watching your inner self mirrored back to you,
and you call it "your life."**

When someone does something to hurt you, there's always a part of you that's complicit with the attack. Always. There's no such thing as a victim or a perpetrator. You project all of your fears, worries, struggles, and unintegrated conflicts onto a neutral world.

When you take responsibility for the way you've been complicit in the bad things that happened to you, you take your power back in a BIG WAY. Saying, "I'm sorry for what I projected on you," is a statement of Truth. Statements of Truth always make you feel stronger.

Forgiving is the Antidote to Projection

The way out of illusion is through FORGIVENESS. There are three distinct steps for forgiveness:

1) You must first become aware that you are projecting your pain onto a neutral world.

2) Realize you are responsible for creating your own painful situations. Let everyone else off the hook for all the things you think they did wrong.

3) You realize there's no one out there to blame. You may start to feel negatively about yourself for the ugly, uncomfortable projections you made for yourself and others all those years.

4) Step two is to forgive yourself for whatever you think you did wrong.

Now you've opened your heart. You're waiting patiently in a state where you don't take anything personally. Now you find you're working with the Divine nature of the Universe to change your delusional beliefs. Ask for help. Ask for help. Ask for help. Higher beings cannot help unless you ask! Stay open and curious to see what they show you. Maybe new insights will be sent to you in your dreams. Maybe new information will come in sudden downloads while you're taking a bath. Maybe new ideas will be sent straight to your heart in the lyrics of a song you hear. **Allow secrets of forgiveness to reveal themselves to you.**

When you learn all the steps of forgiveness, you finally grow up.

Forgiveness is the Best Protector

Forgiveness is more effective than any form of self-protection. This one thought changes everything. Before, in 3D, massive amounts of personal energy were spent using coping mechanism to make sure you were safe, to ward off pain, to stay emotionally armored, and to ensure the success of your future.

In 4D, you don't have to use previous coping mechanisms to stay safe. All you have to do is practice forgiveness. Love and acceptance are your BEST PROTECTORS.

Seeing another as yourself is better than defending yourself. You don't have to argue with others or actively ward off danger. Forgiving is better than hiding, running, lying, or people-pleasing. Judging creates an emotional charge. Instead, accepting somebody exactly as they are removes your emotional charge. Seeing another as yourself breaks down the illusion that you're in danger. You actually aren't, and never were. If you find that you deeply understand this concept, know that you've achieved an climbed the ladder to reach an advanced rung of Fourth Density.

Chapter 16

If You Want to Shift, You Have to Heal

Using 4D Strategies NOW, for Permanent Change

"Fifteen years ago, metaphysics was all about philosophy.
It's no longer enough to just KNOW.
Now is the time in history when we need to
KNOW HOW."

~ Joe Dispenza

Healing is the single most important job you must do in order to shift from Third Density. The transformation from 3D to 4D is your biggest chance to change and heal the lower chakras, so it's important that we discuss the topic in detail.

Healing means replacing misunderstanding with understanding. Healing means replacing darkness with light. Healing means replacing fear with love. Healing means replacing apathy with joy. The word "forgiveness" is the deeper meaning of healing. Forgiveness is to make peace with all the parts of yourself and your world. **Forgiveness reunites everything back together into ONE.** Healing/forgiveness is the act that brings us home to ourselves.

Can I Start the Process of Shifting to 4D Now?

Because Earth is so close to the Great Shift, you don't have to die to engage fourth-density-heart-activation. You don't even have to wait for the Earth to cross through the dimensional gateway. You can do it now. You can "die before you die," as the old Islamic saying goes. 3Ders are awakening their hearts to compassion, cooperation, and equality every day. When it happens to you – there's no way you'll miss it.

To "die before you die" means letting all of your outmoded patterns and beliefs die. It means taking power back from your ego and handing the reins over to your heart. In addition to the word "healing," the process could also be called "clearing", "shadow work," or "consciousness work."

If you really want it, you can attain Fourth Density enlightenment **now**, by doing as much clearing, shadow work, or consciousness work as you can in the time you have.

All density shifts happen WITHIN YOURSELF. The only way to shift is to stop looking out there - to stop looking up at the skies and turn your gaze inwardly. No one is going to rescue you. The extraterrestrials aren't going to come down and fetch you with their ships. The angels won't come take you away. They aren't allowed to. You have to do the work to ascend by yourself.

**If you want to move forward,
you can't get away with NOT facing
ALL the parts of yourself.**

The Key to Unlocking the 4D Gateway

Remember, Section III is acting as a guidebook to power you toward the 4D shift. You don't have to stay in 3D frequencies anymore if you don't want to. The universe is helping you. It is pushing you along. At this point in history, taking one step toward God means He will take 10 toward you. Doing your work to dispel 3D shadows and misperceptions is the focus here. Put your efforts toward cleaning up all the old junk now. Do it with all your heart! Don't look anywhere else. Don't worry about higher realms just yet. Let's get ourselves to the Fourth Density Gateway!

The most important thing you can do to prepare yourself for the shift is to clear your blockages. You must use the winds of love to blow away the fog from your Third Density "Earth Kit." Healing is a word that's become so commonplace that you may not realize how significant it really is. **Healing means removing any resistance to love.** It isn't by force. It is done by gently working with our hurt spots until they willingly surrender open.

What are Blocks to Love?

Blocks are limiting ideas and feelings which stand in the way of Love's natural expression and flow. They may come in the form of **hurt feelings, old grudges, misunderstandings, unwillingness to see innocence in oneself or another, envy, a need to be right, unwillingness to forgive,** and other emotions that cause feelings of contraction.

According to The Law of One, shifting to 4D means learning to live from Love at least fifty-one percent of the time. (James A. McCarty, 1983). Thinking and acting lovingly fifty-one percent of the time is not nearly as easy as one might imagine. Take a moment for honest self-reflection. Consider not only how you treat others, but how you treat YOURSELF. How often do you critique yourself? Beat yourself up? Do you replay conversations over and over again, wishing you'd said things differently? Do you think negative thoughts about your body? Do you think snarky thoughts about other people's appearances or behaviors? Do you judge others' spiritual or moral attainment? Do you compare yourself?

When you do any of these, you are ABANDONING YOURSELF.

You'll know when you're not living from Love if you're hurting, uncomfortable, or frustrated, or if you're depressed, anxious, or experiencing PTSD or OCD. If you feel any of these feelings most of the day, you're probably abandoning yourself.

It's a moment-by-moment spiritual practice to work through the blocks that make us slide toward lower chakra imbalances. *Sliding into forgetfulness* **is a risk - all day, every day.** It is best to stay as mindful as possible in every situation so each life circumstances can be used as practice. I call it "remembering to remember." It's not reasonable to assume that a few positive affirmations "Pollyana-style" can be referred to as healing work. The Universe knows when you're really doing your work toward healing and forgiveness, and when you're not. *A Course in Miracles* **is a great 4D teaching** from which you can learn to practice forgiveness.

What Does Healing Work Look Like?

Healing looks like making peace with yourself. An injured or sick body is not at peace. A resentful, unforgiving heart is not at peace. A confused, mistaken mind is not at peace.

Healing looks like integrating conflict within. When two parts of our psyche are arguing because they don't agree, it causes stress within the being. Re-integrating the two parts back into agreement has an immediate calming effect. By accepting every part of ourselves, imperfections and all, we heal.

Healing looks like reclaiming parts of yourself you've rejected. When you go through painful experiences, parts of yourself can become split off. Trauma can leave you feeling like an unfinished puzzle. It can make you feel like Swiss cheese, with holes in your middle. Hurtful experiences can damage your fragile psyche. You may feel you aren't worthy, you don't fit in, or you don't matter. You may feel shame, guilt, or self-loathing. You may feel victimized, wronged, or run-over.

In an attempt to survive, you may unconsciously reject these painful feelings. You may push the hurt parts down in an attempt to give them safe hiding places. Psychology calls this "dissociation." The rejected parts are DESPERATE for your love. Bringing those lost parts back out into the light is a vital step in preparing yourself for Ascension. In my private practice, I've found that "parts work" (Internal Family Systems Therapy) is an effective and relatively quick way to retrieve rejected parts and to clear trauma. It's part shamanic healing, part psychotherapy. I use it for myself because it makes whatever problem I'm having suddenly seem clear to me. Using "parts work" brings instant insight and immediate release. I love it because it makes me feel empowered. Using parts work gives me control over whether I continue to suffer or not.

Healing looks like remembering Truth. Every aspect of creation holds a bit of distortion (because of our amnesia). Every aspect of creation also holds hidden, innate memories of Original Truth. As a self-healer, you will naturally struggle with whatever places are still distorted. **The *feeling of conflict* is your alarm bell to alert you to the parts that need work.** When you sense which parts of yourself are out of alignment with Truth, it's time to work to contain them within your loving heart-chakra energy. Truths will naturally begin to re-emerge.

Healing looks like forgiving everyone and everything, especially yourself. Forgiveness is one of those things that 3Ders just cannot truly grasp yet. 4Ders are beginning to get it. 5Ders understand forgiveness even more. 6Ders understand the whole picture. Forgiveness is a PROCESS that takes lifetimes for your soul to learn. In fact, you could say that the ENTIRE PURPOSE of a soul's journey through the densities is to learn to **FORGIVE EVERYTHING.** One. Thought. At. A. Time.

Healing is moving into feelings of peace. When you remove the blocks to loving yourself and others, when you practice acceptance and forgiveness, when you replace mis-perception with Truth, when you rejoin all the "parts" that have been hiding out in their separate corners, **you will feel QUIET.** When that peaceful silence descends over your body, you'll feel a Divine Comfort that surpasses any worldly band-aid you might have tried to use. **An overwhelming feeling of Gratitude is the sign that true healing is occurring.** Then joy and love have room to burst open! This is TRUE HEALING.

Healing isn't complicated or complex. It's not secret or mysterious, but it does take training and it takes knowledge of the process. Guidance is needed in order to understand how to work with the ego's persuasive voices. There's only one way we all heal: by transcending our current, distorted state of mind, and shifting to a more Truthful one. If you need help, find a trustworthy guide. *Healing is the most important thing you can do in this life.*

Your Emotional GPS

The way your being tells you whether you're healing or not is through a brilliant system, built right into your body: your EMOTIONS. The system works very simply and with 100% effectiveness. If you feel contracted, it means you're out of alignment with your higher self. If you feel expanded, it means you're in alignment with your higher self. The purpose of your Emotional GPS is to show you **how high or low you're vibrating at any given moment.**

Healing is a process of taking something that hurts, and leading it to a place that doesn't.

To Heal is to Transform a Mis-thought into a True Thought

What is "True Thought?" **When you think a thought that ISN'T in alignment with Truth, you will always feel confusion, difficulty, struggle, anxiety, or depression.** Getting close to *any form of Truth* will always produce feelings of relief, hope, ease, and even bliss.

Confusion is always your sign that you've got a belief that doesn't align with the truth. If you feel confused – stop everything. Ask for help from a higher power to look at the situation again with a more expansive, more compassionate perspective. When you shift your perception just a little bit closer to Love, the confusion will start to dissolve and you'll begin to feel empowered instead.

Feeling Bad = Mis-alignment with your higher self.
Feeling Good = Alignment with your higher self.

The Emotional GPS is set up so that you can easily know when you're off-center in any given moment.

Beware of Pitfalls

There are a few pitfalls you should be aware of in the process of healing. If you're avoiding admitting something to yourself, you won't feel better. **Evasion is pretending you feel good when you don't.** Misleading yourself might bring temporary relief, but it's basically lying to yourself, and 4Ders don't lie to themselves! Besides, you don't want temporary relief. You want permanent relief.

In the end, you can never truly avoid anything. Whatever you avoid will eventually catch up to you. It's better to try to follow your emotional GPS as honestly as you can, NOW. It's ok if you did not know how to do this before. There's always time to begin something new. You haven't lost any time. On your spiritual path, you can never lose anything.

If you're telling yourself Truth, you will never feel worse. Even if the truth SUCKS, it will feel good to admit it. Speaking the smallest Truth brings relief. Being honest is vulnerable. Being vulnerable is a lot more powerful than trying to be "perfect."

Physical, mental and emotional transparency is a 4D skill you're learning, so strive to make it happen now.

Honesty causes a release of pressure.

From this less pressured place, new insights will emerge. Remember, you can't solve a problem with the same belief system from which the problem originated. For instance, if you've been following a spiritual teaching and you don't feel better, it's not the right path for you. Have the courage to try something new.

It's Vital to Apply Healing to the Site of the Wound

If you scrape your knee, does it promote healing to spray anti-bacterial solution on your elbow? Of course not. It's your knee that needs help.

Healing efforts must be applied to the site of the wound. This can be a little tricky. It may appear that a wound is present in the physical body, when in reality, its roots lie in the emotional body. I'm the first to admit that it's difficult to see my own "stuff." I regularly use helpers (therapists, healers, teachers) to assist me in seeing those things I'm blind to. I need help sometimes to see where the wound ACTUALLY is. When I find the location of the wound, my healing efforts are effective. **If I don't locate the true site of the wound, my efforts are in vain.**

It may feel as though the various ways that you can be damaged are endless, but good news! This is not true. Everything in 3D has a finite quality to it, including your inner wounds. There are only a handful of ways that wounding happens within the "Earth-Kit." Once you know what they are, healing will be much less overwhelming.

There are only three possible sites to any wound: your physical body, your emotions, and your mind. Let's compare and contrast each of these sites in detail so you'll have a complete understanding of how to heal yourself.

~ ~ ~ ~ LOCATING PHYSICAL WOUNDS ~ ~ ~ ~ ~

**To heal the BODY,
we must correct structural injuries
and remove physical infections
with our knowledge of 4D Superpowers**

The wounds of the **physical body** are almost always rooted in the first or second chakras. Physical healing consists of learning to make a loving connection with your body, learning to speak its language, and tracking what's happening in real time.

Did you know that your physical body has its own, personal consciousness, apart from your mind? Think of the human body as though it is a separate, individual entity with wisdom of its own. You live within **and** alongside the consciousness of this body. The body has a nervous system which developed over millions of years.

The physical body thinks and behaves on its own, without your conscious awareness. Your body possesses the ability to think and behave at the (approximate) developmental level of a 2-year-old. You will find that it needs to be cared for like a parent caring for a child. Your body loves to be spoken to sweetly. It loves to be doted on. It loves to be held and stroked, massaged and groomed. It needs to trust that you're going to take care of it and keep it safe.

If you want to shift from 3D to 4D, you must master the human "Earth-Kit." Purification of the body is done by learning to listen to your body and give it what it is asking for. **It's called self-care.** Begin in simple ways. If you are tired, rest. If you are sick, take healing medicines and eat nutritious foods. If you are triggered or overwhelmed, give yourself a time-out. If you need touch, be brave enough to ask for safe forms of touch. Ask for help when you need help. Human bodies are wired for connection. We were never meant to "go it alone."

Using 4D Superpowers to Address Physical Ailments

Once you've determined that there's a wound in the body which needs help, you can apply healing medicine to the right place. Since the body is made of dense material, it holds on to your *deeply held, pervasive negative thought patterns or beliefs*. These mis-thoughts make your body sick. **Your physical malady will resolve when you finally grasp the lesson. When you correct the incorrect belief, you will get better.** It may be hard to believe that, but it is a law of the universe.

**Be willing to break your old stuck ideas
about yourself and your world,
for these are what are making you ill.**

Your beliefs hold your body in sickness. Third Density allopathic doctors don't understand this, but Fourth Density alternative healers do. Your physical body is an illusion, albeit a very convincing one! **Because your body is *literally held together by your consciousness*, the cells and the DNA in your body respond to changes in consciousness.** If you are sick or structurally impaired, or injured, begin practicing healing your body with your consciousness. You can do this kind of healing by using visualization, inner child work, Internal Family Systems healing work, and shamanic journeys, to name a few. All are effective ways you can change your *deeply held, pervasive negative thought patterns* with your mind.

You can also heal the body through somatic modalities like EFT (tapping), or somatic trauma release techniques. These physical healing practices are beyond the scope of this book, although I do use them regularly in client sessions.

Humans tend to try to push pain away. All physical beings do it, in fact. It's a natural survival impulse. It may seem counter-intuitive, but **instead of leaning AWAY from your discomforts, if you lean INTO them they will respond positively.**

Let's use the following 4D practices to get an idea of what it's like using your consciousness to heal your physical body.

**** 4D Healing Meditation for a Physical Wound: "The Language Your Body Speaks"*

"Tracking" means observing, listening, and understanding what the body is communicating. Comprehending what's happening in your body requires focus. It is extremely important that you understand that you must become aware of whatever is coming up in the now - in the moment — RIGHT THIS INSTANT. Before you can apply love to a wounded block, you have to know what the blockage is. **The best way to find out is to learn how**

your physical body communicates with you. *The four ways your body will speak to you are **emotion, imagery, sensation, or words.***

Let's say your issue is a headache.

Does your body speak with the language of <u>emotion</u>? *You might notice that when you tune into or "track" the pain in your head, it suddenly brings on a wave of emotion, like sadness, frustration, or maybe anxiety.* <u>**This emotion is your body's attempt to communicate with you.**</u>

Does your body speak with the language of <u>imagery</u>? *When you speak lovingly to your headache, you might suddenly get an image of your dad yelling at you when you were 15.* <u>**This imagery is your body's attempt to communicate with you.**</u> *What does this image tell you? Go with your first instinct and track what's there. Your body is trying to tell you the headaches are connected to the events of that time. If you take care of that 15-year-old within, it could clear those headaches right up. I see this kind of healing happen all the time.*

Does your body speak with the language of <u>sensation</u>? *Perhaps when you speak lovingly to your headache, tears begin to well up, or maybe your neck becomes hot, or your head begins to tingle.* <u>**This sensation is your body's attempt to communicate with you.**</u> *Do a body-scan, or "track" what you find as you move down your body, checking your physical sensations. Tracking your sensation and then forming a caring RELATIONSHIP with those sensory feelings will bring about healing. Working with physical sensations is called "Somatic Release Work."*

Does your body speak with the language of <u>words</u>? *When you tune into or "track" the pain in your head, ask it what it needs. You might hear words such as, "I need an ice pack and a shoulder massage." Or, "I haven't been paying enough attention to the upsetting situation with my boss." Or, "I need more breaks from* my kids." ***These words are your body's attempt to communicate with you.***

It's easy to learn to read the signs your body is giving you when you just tune in and pay attention to yourself. It's not hard to learn to speak the language of your body. 1) Locate the physical pain; 2) face it with care; 3) pay attention to how it's communicating with you. You'll understand a lot. Understanding how your body communicates with you will help you apply the right treatment to the right location, in the right way.

***4D Healing Meditation for a Physical Wound: "Making a Loving Connection"

To make a loving connection with your body, try talking to it. This might seem weird at first but do it anyway. Here's how: gently speak to your body like a mother speaks to her child. "Oh sweetie, your head hurts? I'm so sorry you're feeling pain. I love you, body. I'm so grateful for all you do for me. Your pain matters to me. Tell me what you need." **Your loving speech is a powerful gesture which quickly reaches the wounded places, and signals that they are safe.** It's amazing. You'll feel your body begin to open up to your love before you even make the next move.

Sound too simplistic? Try it.

It's imperative that you learn how your body talks to you, so you can track. After you speak lovingly to your headache, observe how your headache replies to you. Everyone's body speaks with a unique language. If you notice tears, or a sudden change in sensation, emotion, or visual imagery, you're on your way to tracking the core of the problem.

*** 4D Healing Meditation for a Physical Wound: "Transforming Physicality"

(Important Note: The psyche doesn't know the difference between make-believe and reality. When you meditate and use visualization practices to help raise your vibration, the images you see are ACTUALLY HAPPENING in the higher levels. Your body believes they are real. Your mind believes they are real. And because they are real to you, they will heal you.)

If you want the following healing to work, it has to be experienced as real, just like one of those dreams when upon waking, you could even be shaking or crying. The realness is so important that you might not be able to remove your blockages if you don't put all your heart and soul into this practice.

Set a deadline for when you'll expect to turn a small corner with your health. Pick a date - for instance, one week from today. Choose one symptom where you'd like to see improvement. Visualize it as so real that it is changed NOW. Ask yourself, "Who am I without this symptom?" "What does my body feel like without it?" "How has my life changed now that I am without this symptom?"

*Keep at it until you notice the **slightest change** in the communication your body is giving you. It doesn't matter if the body-communication seems to be worse or better. ANY change eventually leads to getting well. Your body could experience somatic sensations like tingling, warmth, heaviness, lightness or numbness. The pain could get worse for a minute, or it might move around. You may feel emotion, get imagery, experience sensation, or hear words.*

Stay with whatever is happening. If you stay with it caringly – IT WILL GET BETTER. Keep talking supportively to your body. *"You're doing well, sweet body. Let's just keep going. We CAN get better. Thank you for communicating with me."*

You might notice a small bit of relief. (If you don't, that's ok. Just keep doing the practice daily until you notice a change.) You could even reach a point where you are pain-free for the moment! THIS IS HUGE! Hold that feeling in your body! Experience being pain-free as exquisitely as you can. Practice the visualization every day until your deadline. **Believe in healing***. If you can do this WITHOUT DOUBTS, you will see a change at or before your deadline date. Remember – this isn't your average "Pollyana-style" positive affirmation.* **This is REAL energy healing.**

Your biggest obstacle with this exercise is working with your doubts. Your doubts are important information pointing directly to your blockages. If you do feel doubts, say, "Thank you for showing me where I'm doubting so I can work to accept and dissolve them." If you can't get past a sticky doubt, go back to practice #1 and make the resistant idea the subject of the healing work.

The practices I just gave you are the very beginning of advanced Fourth Density work which involves shifting timelines using consciousness itself. When you get to 4D, you'll be healing yourself naturally this way all the time.

You DO have the power to learn the language of your body and to consciously heal it. **Your power to heal your body will come when you realize that physical, solid reality isn't what you think it is.** There are some things that are real, and some things that are not real. What is real are those things which never die. The soul is real. The Creator is real. Love is real. **The *creation* is not real.** (The body is a created thing.) It's not what we think it is. It's an illusion. A dream. A holographic image which has been projected outward from your *mind*. Because it's just a hologram, you can heal your body with your consciousness. Practice. Practice. Practice.

~ ~ ~ ~ ~ **LOCATING MENTAL WOUNDS** ~ ~ ~ ~ ~

To heal your MIND,
you must correct your misperceptions.

Wounds of the mind show up as an inability to discern Truth from falsehood. Mental pathology is a confused state where we believe we understand, but we do not. The skew always occurs in the third and fifth chakras. Remember, the lower intellect is a 3D experience, and is part of the third chakra curriculum. The higher intellect is a 5D experience and is part of the fifth chakra curriculum. In healing work, the heart doesn't need healing as often, because the heart IS THE PRIMARY HEALER.

Purifying the mind means learning to
turn wrong perceptions into right perceptions.

One of the best movies ever made, in my opinion, was *The Matrix* (the first film in the series). The Wachowski Brothers, who wrote and directed the movie, must either be Sixth-Density-activated, or they've got some awesome whistle-blower-insiders spoon feeding them certain Universal Truths. **Third Density is almost exactly like the Matrix.** Go back and watch the film again

245

and really think about how humanity's collective consciousness has created a "mental program." Think about how we are all agreeing to run the mental program with our subconscious, collective consent. Now, I can't say that I buy into the part of the film where human bodies are being kept alive in goo-filled, fake uteruses while our minds are tricked into believing we're living real lives in an imitation world. No. That part is Hollywood. But really pay attention to the idea that **the matrix is a world made up of pure THOUGHT**. In the matrix, and in your life, what you believe is what you experience. If you could embody this knowledge, you could have the same powers as Neo!

If you want in on the greatest secret of ascension, here it is: **We're making this whole place up in our minds.** Neo knew this. Once he understood what "reality" was, he was able to transcend the 3D laws of physics. How did he do that?

Neo understood that the 3D laws of physics didn't exist. Only his BELIEF in 3D limitation existed.

So, purifying your mind is all about waking up from your denial, taking the red pill, and realizing that YOU have all the power in the Universe. It's just a matter of knowing how to use it!

How does one purify the mind enough to break the spell of the 3D Matrix? There are many practices. Here are a few:

*** 4D Healing Meditation for a Mental Wound: "Changing Destructive Beliefs"

Choose a belief that you truly think is fixed and unchanging. For example, "I'll never meet the mate of my dreams." Focus your mind on this thing. Now say, "This is a belief my subconscious adopted many years ago to protect me from vulnerable feelings in the best way it knew how. I choose now to open to the idea that this belief isn't really fact." Introducing a freeing thought will instantly begin to work on the subconscious. **Speaking ANY bit of Truth will start the process of accessing the whole Truth.** It starts opening up ancient, latent memories within you that know that nothing is "real" but Love. Everything else is NOTHING.

Now imagine the belief as a colored bubble living inside your energy field. Zoom in and see the tiny bits of information that make up the belief. If you have a belief that you can't attract or keep a good mate, how did that come into being? Did someone tell you that? Was it a defense you made against pain? Become aware of the way your belief has shaped your life. How did it affect your dating experiences in high school and college, or as a young adult? How does this belief affect relationships now? How does it affect your self-image or self-esteem? Do you have secondary beliefs floating around it like, "Because I don't have a wonderful partner, it must mean that there's something wrong with me. It must mean I'm unlovable." Or, "Because I haven't had a good track record with partners, I'll be alone forever." Become aware of how each of these secondary beliefs shape the way you feel about yourself.

Beliefs, just like matter, are made up of energy. Each one of those belief bubbles living in your energy field is controlled by your consciousness. Your consciousness created them, and your consciousness can dissolve them. (This has actually been proven in *scientific experiments many times over:* **particles of both matter AND energy respond to the consciousness of the observer.)**

Look at your bubble. Talk to your belief. "I'm aware of you here inside me. I have an inkling where you came from. I know you're not a True Perception, and I would like to work together toward change." **Remember – nothing changes by force. Change happens through loving the thing back into wholeness.** *Respect it, and it will respect you back, and it will do as you ask. Ask the belief bubble to work with you. CHECK TO SEE IF IT IS WILLING! You must work together with the parts of yourself. If the belief is too resistant, you'll have to make friends with it first before you'll get it to buy into your ideas.*

If the belief is willing to work with you, make a request that it change in some small way. Ask the bubble of belief to become softer in its stubborn, rigid thought process. Ask yourself if it might be possible to consider that the belief can change. Visualize a little crack in your bubble that let's fresh, new light in. "Maybe it's NOT true that I'm unlovable. Maybe it's NOT true that I am unable to secure a good relationship." Maybe something else is true. Be open to new possibilities. Ask your belief bubble to give you an outward sign that's it's willing to soften its ideas by changing its color. If it is willing to soften, use your 4D superpowers (which these exercises are all about), to see if the bubble changes color. **If you notice a color change, take that as an absolute signal that there's been a shift on the template level.**

The key here is that one small change leads to another. *That's why we start with such small steps. If the belief bubble has shown you it is willing to soften its thought system, then ask if it is willing to take it up a notch. Imagine what your life would be like if the belief bubble gave up its strangle-hold enough to allow a new feeling into your awareness. (Be willing to accept small clues here. Give it some time. Don't give up just because a new lover doesn't show up tomorrow.) Use your wildest imagination to* *conjure up what your new life might feel like. Really go all out! Imagine a scene with a new special person. Feel, see, taste, hear, and smell your new reality. The more real you make your scenario, the more potent it will be in its effectiveness. The most important part is to IMAGINE what this would actually feel like!* **The belief bubble wants to please you!** *After all – it went to all this trouble to protect your heart all these years. It wants to please you because it's part of you.*

You can't do this wrong. This experience is just practice/play, and is going to be unique for everyone. The act of getting THIS INVOLVED with your belief, befriending it, understanding it's experience, remembering when it showed up in your life, how it was trying to protect you, asking it to change, seeing how it responds to your requests.... This is the real energy work. You are working directly with creation through your thoughts.

Within the next few days, be curious to see if you notice ANY SLIGHT CHANGE IN YOUR PERCEPTIONS. Be willing for the change to be slight. You might feel an emotion you haven't felt in many years coming back to life within you. Maybe it's a feeling of hope or a feeling of being in love. Perhaps an attractive stranger checks you out in the grocery store. It's probably nothing you'd act on, but the PRESENCE OF THE FEELING is what you're interested in. These are small tastes from the universe showing you that you're on the right track. They are little signs that you've shifted something within.

If you're skeptical, this practice is likely not to prove anything to you, **because you'll only see change when you believe in the process.** Why? Because your consciousness rules what you experience. If your consciousness says, "This is hooey," then you'll get hooey.

Pay attention to the tiny ways the world opens up to you after you play these mental games. Nothing is coincidence. Open to notice all the signs. **Once your limiting and painful belief bubble sees the light of Truth, it won't stop developing unless you stop it.** You'll begin to see change more and more.

*** 4D Healing Meditation for the Mind: "Affecting Collective Reality"

(Reminder: The psyche doesn't know the difference between make-believe and reality. When you meditate and use visualization practices to help raise your vibration, the images you see are actually HAPPENING in the higher levels. Your body believes they are real. Your mind believes they are real. And because they are real to you, they will heal you.)

Bad things that happen seem real, but in reality – they are just thought bombs going off everywhere. Next time you hear of something awful – like a viral pandemic wreaking havoc the world over, take pause and do some work. Close your eyes and turn the scene around. Remember, nothing changes by force. Things change when they are loved back to peace. Imagine little viral-beings surrounded in bubbles of love, protected away so they can't hurt people. Instead of fearing or hating them, try to feel a sense of compassion for all the little viruses. **You may have to do some work on your own beliefs about the pandemic before you can accept and love the virus-beings.** *Acceptance can't be faked. Your sense of compassion must be true and real for it to work. Imagine the viral-beings feeling cared for. Imagine giving the tiny beings permission and encouragement to begin evolving at their own level of consciousness. All of creation has an impulse to spiritually evolve. (The virus WANTS to evolve and it will appreciate your encouragement!) Imagine the little viruses begin to understand a different way to get their needs met. Instead of* *making their hosts sick, they learn that they can turn toward their creator to get their needs met.*

Be the spiritual teacher for the less aware soul.

Go all out in your visualization. Through the power of your love, teach the virus to exist through different means. Teach them that Instead of invading human cells, the viruses can choose to find alternative methods to get their needs met. **When 4D consciousness is used, there is always "another way."**

See the cities clean and perfect. See no trace of any virus in anyone's body. Visualize the people smiling and happy. See empty, stress-free hospitals. Imagine the news stations having nothing to report but human interest pieces that exude feelings of hope and human-caring. See government leaders experiencing sudden changes in their hearts, committing themselves to full transparency. Imagine citizens being told the truth. See people coming together, WEARING NO MASKS, hugging each other with love and trust. There is a complete absence of fear or panic.

Believe it's true. Don't let doubt get its foot in the door.

That last exercise may have seemed fantasia-like. These exercises are simply suggestions to play with which will help you heal schisms in your body, emotions and mind. The feelings and experiences you have when you are doing these meditations are little tastes of what it'll be like in 4D. With your consciousness, you'll be doing your part to energize a new collective matrix where wounds won't form at all anymore.

~ ~ ~ ~ ~ LOCATING EMOTIONAL WOUNDS ~ ~ ~ ~ ~

To heal your Emotional Body,
you must seek out the things that 'erk' you,
then learn to fully accept them as they are.

Emotional wounds are always rooted in the second, third or fourth chakras. Emotional healing consists of emotional nurturing, emotional safety, and person-to-person connection.

Wounds in the emotional body usually hide more deeply than those of the physical body, and therefore can be confusing, seem more mysterious, and might even feel superficially scary. It's ok. You just need to understand what is there. Then you won't be afraid.

If you want to shift to 4D consciousness, you must learn all about your emotions, and then learn to manage them. Change doesn't happen by force, but by gentle nudges from your heart. Managing emotions isn't done by using old-world rigidity and will-power, where one pushes down his or her feelings in order to appear strong or refined. Fourth Density purification works in a whole new way. You must find the source of the emotional upset, accept it, bring love to it, **and then *make a different choice.***

Humans in Third Density carry a lot of fear. Because you don't know what it is you are truly afraid of, you project your fears and anxieties out onto your exterior world. You feel afraid of burglars, authority figures, political figures, pandemics, snakes, terrorists, your family, running out of money, being alone, the boogieman, and you're afraid nobody likes you. **But what it all boils down to is the fact that you are afraid of WHAT IS INSIDE OF YOU.** Why? Because you don't really *know* what is inside of you. The unknown can be terrifying. **If you knew your inner landscape, you would not be scared of anything anymore.**

Emotional pathology is always caused by fear.

Doing your shadow work means getting to know your inner landscape. Healing an emotional wound is a process of **re-turning** toward yourself instead of recoiling away from ourself.

*** *4D Healing Meditation for an Emotional Wound:*
"Awareness and Self-Love"

Become aware. *When you catch yourself feeling emotionally triggered - pause. Name the specific emotion: fear, hurt, anger, grief. Admit that there are big parts of yourself that you don't know about yet. Admit that you still don't fully understand the power of love and consciousness to heal you. (There is no shame in this. Awareness is an essential first step.)*

Make a CHOICE *to begin again. Say to yourself, "I know I have a lot to overcome, but I know there is something wonderful on the other side. I want to step out of this old way which hasn't been making me happy. I want to try something new."*

ASK for help. *Beginners aren't ready to do emotional healing on their own. This is a learned process. Ask for help from God, your angels, and your higher self. Ask for help by reading new books you wouldn't have considered reading before. Ask for help by seeing a conscious therapist or healer. Ask for help by talking to awakened friends, going to a new workshop, or taking a class. Ask for help by learning to meditate. (The guided*

253

meditations on my website and my YouTube channel will help. Don't worry if you don't know how to meditate. The guided meditations themselves are designed to teach you as you go). Be open for help to come in unexpected ways.

Use self-love to hold and contain yourself. Accept yourself exactly where you are. Whatever you're feeling, even if it's embarrassing, shameful, or ugly, realize that all of your feelings are NORMAL. We ALL feel complex webs of emotion. You often feel something, and then you hate yourself for feeling it.

Imagine your heart can grow large enough to encompass and surround all those places that hurt. Let your heart HUG those bad feelings with compassion. **Let those feelings act-out as BIG as they want to!** Let them scream dirty words! Let them be messy. The heart doesn't care if they're ugly. The heart loves everything as it is. Be patient and notice if those painful feelings slowly begin to calm down as the heart does its compassion-healing-work. There is only kind of medicine for emotional wounds: full acceptance as they are right now. **Flood these places with love.**

*** 4D Healing Meditation for an Emotional Wound: "Creating a New Past" or "Re-writing History"

You've just been reminded of a painful event from the past. Take a minute and focus. Close your eyes and picture the situation. See the details of the location. What does the room look like? Do you remember any smells? This may not be comfortable, but we must recall it in order to heal it. Leaning INTO our discomfort is the way to change it.

Imagine going backwards in time to the moment just before the scary event. Now imagine a special person appearing *right in front of your eyes. This special person is your wise-future-self from a higher realm! Imagine what he or she looks like. Is she wearing all white? Is he glowing? See his or her face. See their shining eyes beaming with love for you. Your future-self knows you better than anyone in the Universe. Feel loved and cared for by this wise being standing before you.*

Now imagine that the mental movie of the upsetting event is beginning. Watch as your wise-future-self stands DIRECTLY BETWEEN YOU AND THE PAINFUL SITUATION WHICH IS OCCURRING. Look into his or her eyes. Do not look away. Imagine that your loving future-self is holding up his or her arms to block your view of the hurtful event. Imagine that they are placing a prayer-spell on the scene so that you can no longer understand the words — all you're hearing is a foreign language! Listen! You only hear babble. Instead, listen to your wise-future-self speak to you about delightful things! Become absorbed in the experience you and your wise-future-self are having. Just allow the upsetting situation to carry on in the background. You are now barely aware of the drama going on. You are only aware of the blissful feelings that you are having with your guardian.

You are re-writing history.

After a little while, let your wise-future-self take your hand and walk you away from the event. Talk with him or her about fun, happy things. Imagine going to get ice-cream together. Go play outside. Jump on the bed. Put on your favorite 80's song and dance. Do anything you want to do that's really, really joyful! Feel how happy you are with this wise, loving, adult-caretaker. You are so well cared for. You have everything you need. Feel and experience the feelings. It's GOOD, right?

You just created a new past or re-wrote history. If the memory happens to cross your mind in the future, you may still be able to remember some of the events that happened, but probably not as clearly as before. The emotions surrounding the situation will be muted. Because of the nature of the quantum universe, your soul can do all kinds of magical things using its consciousness. It can even change details of past traumatic events. Believe it, practice it, and feel it.

A Word about Emotional Trauma

When traumatic memories get triggered, your body will drench itself in adrenaline. When you're in this state, your conscious mind, or executive functioning goes offline as the body shunts all its efforts into protecting itself through fight, flight, freeze, or fawn. It puts you into a child-like, self-focused state, where you become incapable of higher forms of communication. No longer are you capable of seeing any other side of the story. No longer are you capable of having compassion for another. All you're capable of is fighting for your own safety. It's all happening in the brain. Your pre-frontal cortex has been kicked offline, and you're functioning from the amygdala or the reptilian brain instead. This kind of trigger happens more often than most people are aware of. Most humans have experienced a great deal of trauma – just from being here on this 3D planet.

I Call Earth "The PTSD Planet."

Trauma gets in the way of normal daily functioning. When PTSD rears its ugly head it is vital to learn to care for yourself properly if you want to progress to Fourth Density.

If you have a history of trauma, it's a good idea to seek out treatment. Trauma usually cannot be healed completely by yourself. If you want to take the first steps, you can educate yourself with books, audios, and online courses; however, humans need a caring, safe, well-trained "other" to reach the place where the trauma lives. When we're beginners, we need another person to help us form a search party so the traumatized part of you can be rescued and led back to safety. **If the trauma was inflicted in relationship with another person - it must be healed in relationship with an experienced, caring other.**

You can begin the process of helping yourself in some ways. Step number one: **CREATE A SAFE PLACE.** This means different things to different people. It could be a safe place in your mind where you can retreat when life gets scary or stressful. It could be a literal place you can visit, like your bedroom, a beautiful chapel, a beach, etc. It might just mean walking away from a volatile situation. It may mean taking a break from a friendship. It could mean going no-contact with your family. The point is to get a *lengthy* retreat in order to put a space between you and the danger. Your traumatized nervous system needs the break in order to begin to heal.

There are other steps for healing trauma which are beyond the scope of this book. Healing trauma isn't easy, but going through the process of healing it is a heck of a lot better than living with PTSD every day for the rest of your life. Get the help you need. It's an act of self-love.

Do You Want to Get the Hell Out of 3D?

When you open to new realities that these exercises induce, you're beginning your Fourth Density training curriculum. **You don't have to master them yet, but you do have to believe if you want to shift.** The catch is: it can't be falsified. If you still doubt, you have to work on the doubt first before you can continue on. Pretending your way past doubts only makes things worse.

If there are places that are still in shadow, skepticism, or disbelief, places that still cause you to feel or think negatively, go back to the very first practice. **Never skip over anything.** Every tiny part of yourself deserves to be seen, heard, and understood. Even the doubting parts! Every single part of your story longs to be re-written into a better one. Each part of you, including your own feelings, sensations and reactions, deserve to be loved back to rightness and balance.

"But isn't this practice really just playing make-believe?"

Well, YES, actually. **The matrix we've collectively created doesn't know the difference between reality and imagination.** Whatever you believe, the matrix will project back onto the movie screen of your life. In my hypnotherapy counseling work, my clients and I spend a LOT of time doing this kind of imagination-creation work together through hypnosis. I regularly see pervasive patterns of pain quickly dissolve. Once you know HOW, it becomes easy. Not to mention FUN! **Then your job becomes doing these exercises in every charged situation you encounter.** Every day.

Doing these exercises in every charged situation, every day is the purpose of your life. We all get triggered. The mark of improvement toward 4D is how quickly you catch yourself. Don't waste time. Don't waste your opportunity to heal and purify yourself.

Do you want to rest?
Or do you want to ascend and get out of here?

It's worth reminding you again that all sickness begins and ends in the mind. **It is the misunderstanding of Truth which**

causes your body, emotions, or mind to become sick. What is a "miracle" other than discovering a clean, pure Truth under layers of 3D thought-grime? When you shift your thinking from fear to Love, miracles occur. Pull out the spray cleaner and some old rags, and let's get to work.

*Note: On my website, PaigeBartholomew.com, you will find more recorded guided meditations. For some people, it is easier to be led in a meditation than to read one. These audio recordings will open your heart and mind, and begin to heal your body. Many of my clients report not knowing how to meditate. When they listen to my guided meditations they tell me how surprised they are that simply following along has helped them learn to meditate on their own.

Chapter 17

Surrender

Awakening to What You ALWAYS Were
Or
The Last Step the Shift Out of Third Density into Fourth Density

"Stop.
Open up.
Surrender to the beloved blind silence.
Stay there until you see that
you're looking at the light with infinite eyes."
~ Jalaluddin Rumi

While making a consciousness shift from one density to the next may sound like just about the coolest thing you can imagine doing, we must also be aware that The Great Ascension carries with it something unavoidable:

LOSS.

Before you can move cleanly into Fourth Density, you must go through a shedding process. **You have to let go of everything you've become attached to in your current station,** all your grand ideas, ways of thinking, ways of living, ways of loving, ways of relating, your stories of your past, the pain you hold onto – they all have to be surrendered. It's not possible to enter into the realm of a higher station without first shedding the garments of the old. We must cross over the density threshold in a fresh, pure and clean state of being.

Transitioning from one density to the next is a bit like dying. Perhaps that's why the Mayan culture and the teachings of other sacred cultures talk about the Great Awakening as a process of death.

A man named John wrote the story of the apocalypse in the Bible, which foretold of great battles that will occur between Light and Dark in the final days of third density. The story was his interpretation of a dream. In the story, the battles, which were between good and evil, are metaphors that describe conflicts old as humanity itself. The apocalypse tells us of many battles and horrors, such as fires, earthquakes, droughts, famines, nuclear blasts, etc. that will occur. John wrote that life on earth will be nearly destroyed. (This is why we wonder if we are now in "the final days.")

John reports that the final battle will take place in a field near Jerusalem. It is predicted by the author that the war between the good forces and evil forces would destroy all the soldiers, families, and cities, and life itself. In the story, Jesus will appear in the sky "in all his glory!" He will rebuke the evil forces, and command the fighting to cease. In the tale, as soon as Jesus speaks, the war ends. Throngs of angels along with lightworkers and people of the Love will gather and feel the fourth density gateway open. The bliss will be immeasurable.

Satan, or the Dark One, as he is sometimes known, immediately knew he had been vanquished. He realized that all his greed, all his pride, and vanity could never win against the forces of goodness and love.

In the apocalypse story, after Christ vanquishes Satan to Antarctica, or wherever, there will be 100 years of peace. 4Ders will stay with Jesus on a peaceful earth. This will be the final act of the ascension! It is the ultimate story of fourth density overcoming third density. It will be clear that love (the 4D way) ultimately wins over misunderstanding and shadow (the 3D way).

The battles represent the struggle within ourselves to let go of the old and to surrender to something wholly new and unknown.

In Islam, the concept of Jihad is widely misunderstood by non-Muslims. Literally translated, Jihad means "Holy War." The deep and holy meaning of Jihad is to make war with the ego inside the self. **To overcome the ways of the lower self is the holiest of all wars.**

Killing another human being for the sake of religion can only be a gross distortion of the meaning of Jihad. Mohammad could never have meant this. Mohammad was a knower. He knew the realms of 4D, 5D, 6D and possibly beyond. When Mohammad talked about making jihad, he meant to make war with the lower self for the sake of one's relationship with God.

263

Jihad is a beautiful thing. Jihad is required if we want to move forward.

How to Surrender

Whenever you find yourself feeling hurt, triggered, miffed, frustrated, furious, confused, sad, lonely, jealous, blameful, hopeless, or longing... TAKE IT TO GOD (or your favorite angel, prophet, or guide).

Taking a feeling or thought to God means turning toward something higher than ourselves, and saying, "I don't know what to do with this. Please help me manage it."

When I do my personal surrender meditation practice, I lie down and close my eyes. I feel my discomfort as clearly as I can. I give it name. The discomfort usually really hurts at first and sometimes I feel resistance to doing the practice, but I know the relief is bound to come if I go ahead with it. I become aware of the imaginary stories I created because of the pain. I see that none of the stories are helping my life. **My ego has tried everything on God's green earth except for the one thing that will work: SURRENDER.**

I usually find that I drop my head in self-disappointment when I realize that I could have surrendered all along. I feel sad that I've wasted so much time. Finally, I turn toward God and ask Him to hold the weight of the feeling for me.

Next, I visualize myself lifting my all of my delusional, dramatic stories upward, and place them into God's hands. There, I let it go. I let God have it. **I make a commitment to stop thinking about it.** I make an intention: if my puny mind picks it back up and starts turning it over and over again, trying to find a solution, I will STOP. I will say, "God, I'm doing it again. I gave this to you to figure out and I don't want to pick it back up after I've already surrendered it. I don't want to play with this problem anymore because it HURTS."

Then I leave it for God. I wait in STILLNESS. I trust that God knows what God is doing. I don't allow myself to think about it again. Eventually, I begin to receive some new insight that I didn't see before. Sometimes it takes 5 minutes, sometimes a few days. **It always works, but only if I really and truly stop struggling with it.** This is the true meaning of the holy war, or the Jihad. It means giving up our human stories we made up. It's not easy because we've been practicing the opposite procedure our whole lives. But the step by step process of surrendering everything in your life is what causes you to "shift."

This practice takes trust. I trust that God, and the higher beings of light know better than I do. I also trust that EVERYTHING in this created world is meaningless. **I don't want to play games with meaningless situations.** I would prefer to surrender all that garbage.

If I've *truly* given my painful thoughts to God, new answers come quickly. New knowing arrives to show me how to handle the stressor. New awareness lands within me to teach me how to behave in the situation.

Doing this practice as regularly as I can remember (every day, I hope) teaches me how to live in the present. I don't have to fret or worry about anything. Through SURRENDER, I simply allow the Universe to lead me through my challenges, and to show me where to take my next step. It's fabulously freeing.

When I look back at my youth, I see a young person who did not know how to surrender completely. She suffered A LOT. Now, I'm tired of that way of living. I want to be free of suffering, and I know I can't fake the process of surrendering. I have to do my work authentically and regularly. My ego needs to be told, "No," and I need to make sure it obeys. I want my ego to go to the time-out-chair.

I thank My Inner Soul Map, and all the enlightened beings who came before me, for teaching me how to walk on my spiritual path. I thank them for teaching me how to get to Peace. Peace is available for you if you desire it. It takes one thing to get it. Full, total, radical surrender: in every moment, in every situation, and for every problem.

As we make the holy war within ourselves, we should expect that it will feel painful and messy. Even experienced practitioners still feel pain. It's called being human. Transitioning from one density to the next is not a painless process. We are literally required to pass through the eye of a needle. We can't take our possessions with us. We can't take our emotional attachments with us. We can't take our grievances with us. The only thing we can take with us is our essential self. It's necessary to purify ourselves to the point of **empty willingness.** This is true surrender.

So be compassionate with yourself. Spiritual work is demanding. But staying stuck in your old ways is more painful than letting it go.

I invite you to let it all go. Surrender yourself to what is higher.

Take your chance right now. Don't put this off. The 4D gateway is open NOW. GO!

"There is no life like the life of a true seeker."

~ Sidi Mohammad Al Jamal, Sufi Master

Chapter 18

The Great Shift

The Greatest Show on Earth!

"Once you have a glimpse of the whole,
life becomes unquestionable.
Question it now.

Once your head opens up to the existence,
meditation becomes impossible.
Meditate now."

~ Saroj Aryal

Many religious texts, ancient stories, and modern soothsayers tell us there is a great shift happening on Planet Earth. I agree.

Since I was a child, I knew that I incarnated into this life to witness something cosmic and grand. I didn't know how to conceive of such a thing as a child; I suppose I was too young to have any framework for it. Back then, it was still just a feeling within me. I used to spend hours asking my mother about God, angels, Jesus, magic, other dimensions, interstellar beings, black holes, past lives, quantum physics, the Loch Ness Monster, and all sorts of mysterious things. When my mother and I talked about those things, those were the moments when I felt the most ALIVE!

As I grew up and begin to try out new spiritual paths, to read ancient, holy texts, and to experiment with alternative religious practices, I began to get back in touch with the part of myself that *knew*. It is an ancient part of me, and a part that has always *known*. It has always known who I am, where I sit within creation, and where I sit with my Creator. I was born with my soul memories intact. It's been important for me to bring that "knowing part" into the forefront, so that I may live from it.

The older I got, the more conscious my memories became. They created a clearer picture of The Humanity Shift I was born to witness. I didn't know all the details, but I knew that it was about human evolution. I knew that there would be a great change for our species, one in which people would swiftly realize what they were unable to understand before. I knew it would be a leap from the ego to the heart. I knew that many beings from higher densities were here to help ... both embodied, and of the spirit.

I knew all of this before I ever picked up a single book about the Great Shift.

When I finally found the first books that actually talked about the ascension, I cried for weeks, because they ignited old visions, pictures, and wisps of memories that I had forgotten how to interpret. As I started reading voraciously, I began to instinctively understand how to interpret my knowings from the time before my birth. My family heard whoops and hollers from the next room as I read pieces of information that jogged my memories. Those memories had been just under the threshold of my conscious mind, then they came back to life. Before, I was only able to SENSE the memories, but I started LIVING the memories!

This is how it can happen for you, too. When you read something that sends shivers down your body, has a "ring of Truth" to it, makes you stop in your tracks, speechless, or it causes you to cry, these are all common reactions to remembering the Truth of what you already know. The veil of forgetting is strong here in Third Density planet Earth. Your amnesia here causes all kinds of problems. But once you "remember", it feels nothing less than AWE-INSPIRING!

Ask For Help

Ask for help in remembering. Your higher self is more powerful than you can imagine. All you have to do is ask the right questions, and the universe will begin to reveal its secrets to you.

What does it mean, "Ask the RIGHT questions?" I'm sure at some point in time, you've experienced praying for something but felt as though you were not heard or answered. The reason is this: **higher beings and your own higher-self will not acknowledge *questions asked from your ego*.** You must purify your body, your heart, and your mind, then think hard about the question you really want to ask. If you ask with an open and sincere heart, you'll hear your answer more clearly.

Another reason you sometimes do not receive an answer, even when you've asked sincerely, is that **you are afraid to hear what you've asked for.** You may *think* you're ready for the answer, but what if you're subconsciously aware that the answer could crater your entire belief system? Do you still want that answer? What if the answer could break your heart, or change your whole life in a way you don't prefer? Are you sure you still want that answer, even if the costs could be very high?

No question is left unanswered. However, **an answer may be dressed in a veil.** When you are ready, and you are unafraid of hearing the hard truth, you can remove the veil and see your answer clearly. If you've made it to chapter 18 of this book, then you are brave. You are one of the very few people who values truth over comfort, and who wants to "know".

Carl Jung said, "Until you make the unconscious conscious, it will direct your life and you will call it fate." Soul evolution is all about "making the unconscious conscious." Soul evolution is all about having courage to look at what you are, not just what you want to be. **It's about spending time in quiet meditation with the Divine energies of the cosmos, asking the right questions with a sincere heart, and being fearlessly prepared to receive the answers that are given to you.**

Some people wonder, "Why don't the higher beings just appear to humanity so that everyone can know we're not alone?" The answer is obvious: too many humans are afraid, and too many don't want the real information. Too many humans want what's going to feel comforting, but don't necessarily want the Truth. They want to stay UNCONSCIOUS. When we, as a collective, decide to overcome our fears and open to the Truth, even if it seems scary, we will SEE WONDROUS THINGS!

The Shift

The Great Shift is upon us. Those who have done their inner work and have opened their hearts to love and forgiveness will see their dreams come true. It's already happening. Are you seeing miracles yet?

I believe humanity will continue to open in small bursts, not all at once, at least for now. Enjoy the heart opening! Enjoy the feeling of expansion! Enjoy the tiny drops of disclosure by our governments! Enjoy watching grassroots movements come together and work toward better living for everyone! Enjoy the insights that come into your life every day – through your dreams, through your friends, through speakers and books, through songs, through prayer, and through direct perception from your higher self.

Trust that the shift is inevitable. Once humanity hits critical mass, the Earth will transition through the 4D gateway and our lives will change forever.

Take a break from looking upward at the heavens for angels, higher beings, or UFOs. Beware of wanting to possess dazzling talents like automatic writing, bending spoons, or remote viewing. **Instead, look into your soul, your innermost being, find out what's there, and surrender. Lay your heart down at the feet of God.**

The shift is happening WITHIN YOU. The gateway is opening for you as a direct response to the state of your CONSCIOUSNESS.

You have so much to contribute, just being YOU. **The true you wants to emerge!** It wants to fly! Open your heart and let everything go! Don't be afraid! Let the world change! Be brave! Don't hang on! Leave all your expectations behind!

You are a deeply treasured, vital part of this ascension process. Fourth density is the Garden realm. There, you are an exquisite bloom which blossoms continually as you learn to love more and more. The Universe needs your soul's specific fragrance! The Garden is waiting for you!

You are a brilliant diamond that deeply yearns to be polished by the presence of God. There is love waiting for you that's beyond anything you've ever felt before. This love will fill your being so that there's no more suffering and no more questioning. The Garden is your birthright. This Garden reveals the pure beauty of God - which is who you are! You ARE the LOVE you want so badly. You ARE the PEACE you long for so much. You ARE more BEAUTIFUL than you have ever believed. **YOU ARE WORTH ALL THE WORK IT TAKES TO GO THROUGH THE SOUL MAP, and to travel back home again, into the arms of your beloved.** YOU are the reason for all of it.

**The Universe knows what it is doing.
YOU ARE THE UNIVERSE.**

Relevant Ascension Resources

A Course in Miracles
www.ACIM.org
Books: *A Course in Miracles, Workbook for Students, Manual for Teachers*

Scott Mandelker
www.ScottMandelker.com
Books: *From Elsewhere, Universal Vision*

Carla Rueckert/ Don Elkins / LL Research
www.llResearch.org
www.lawOfOne.info
Books: *The Law of One: The Ra Material (Books 1-5), A Wanderer's Handbook, Voices of the Confederation*

Corey Goode
www.SphereBeingAlliance.com
TV Show: Cosmic Disclosure on the Gaia Network

Bentinho Massaro
www.BentinhoMassaro.com

Dr. David Hawkins
www.veritaspub.com
Books: *Power vs. Force, Truth vs. Falsehood, Transcending the Levels of Consciousness*, and more....

The Power Path
www.ThePowerPath.com

Books: *The Michael Handbook, Encounters with Power: Adventures and Misadventures of the Shamanic Path of Healing*

David Wilcock

www.DivineCosmos.com
TV Shows: Wisdom Teachings, Cosmic Disclosure on the Gaia Network
Books: *The Synchronicity Key, The Ascension Mysteries, The Source Field Investigations, Awakening in the Dream*

Marianne Williamson

www.Marianne.com
Books: *A Return to Love, Spiritual Keys to Healing Anxiety and Depression*, and more…

Patricia Pereira

Books: *Songs of the Arcturians, Eagles of the New Dawn*

Michael Newton, PH.D

www.NewtonInstitute.org
Books: *Life Between Lives, Journey of Souls, Destiny of Souls*

Zoev Jho

Books: *E.T. 101*

Delores Cannon

www.DeloresCannon.com
Books: *The Three Waves of Volunteers and The New Earth*, and more…

Brian Weiss

http://www.brianweiss.com
Books: *Miracles Happen, Many Lives Many Masters, Through Time Into Healing, Only Love is Real*, and more….

Shadhuliyya Sufi Center
> www.SufiMaster.org

Llewellyn Vaughn Lee
> https://www.goldensufi.org
> Books: *Spiritual Ecology, For Love of the Real, Love is a Fire: The Sufi's Mystical Journey Home,* and more...

IN5D Greg Prescott
> www.in5d.com

Eben Alexander
> http://ebenalexander.com/
> Books: *Proof of Heaven, Living in a Mindful Universe*

Ken Wilbur
> www.Integrallife.com
> www.KenWilbur.com

Jeremy Huttenberg
> Book: *Non-Violent Communication: Effective Guide to Relationships Psychology, Avoid Conflict and Connect with People*

Master Physicist Nassim Haremein
> www.resonancescience.org

Foster Gamble
> www.thethrivemovement.com

George Van Tassel
> www.integraron.com
> Books: *The Council of Seven Lights. Into This World and Out Again,* and more...

.

William Henry

www.williamhenry.com

Books: *The Watchers, Oracle of the Illuminati, Mary Magdalene The Illuminator: The Woman Who Enlightened the Christ*, and more….

Gaia TV

www.gaiatv.com or www. Amazon.com

New Age media video streaming focusing on topics of awakening, consciousness, transformational thought, fringe-science and yoga

Tara Brach

www.tarabrach.com

Podcasts on Sound True, Apple and Spotify

Books: *Radical Compassion* and *Radical Acceptance*

Works Cited

As-Shadhili, S. M.-J.-R. (1994). *Music of the Soul.* Petaluma, Ca: Sidi Muhammad Press.

Campbell, J. (2018). *The Hero's Journey.* Joseph Campbell Foundation, Ed 2.

Childre, D. (1991). *HeartMath Institute.* Retrieved from www.HeartMath.org

Elaine Aron, P. (1996). *The Highly Sensitive Person.* New York, NY: Broadway Books.

Elkins, R. &. (1984). *The Law of One Series.* Atglen, PA, PA: Whitford Press.

Entertainment, G. V. (Director). (2013 - present). *Wisdom Teachings by David Wilcock* [Motion Picture].

Haramein, N. (2004). *Resonance Science Foundation.* Retrieved from *www.rresonancescience.org*

Haramein, N. (2019). *Cosmometry.* Cosmometria Publishing

Henry, W. (2015). *The Watchers: Lost Secrets of Ascension, Resurrection and Perfection.* Hendersonville, TN: Scala Dei.

Henry, W. (2016, 06 06). *The Awakened Soul: Lost Science of Ascension.* Retrieved from William Henry: http://www.williamhenry.net/2016/06/the-awakened-soul-the-lost-art-and-science-of-ascension-and-the-ultimate-yoga-experience/

Hicks, E. a. (2006). The Law of Attraction: The Basics of the Teachings of Abraham. Hay House; 1st edition

Jung, C. (1967) The Philosophical Tree. Routledge and K. Paul.

Phillips, D. T. (2009, 12 23). *NASA.* Retrieved from NASA Science BETA: https://science.nasa.gov//science-news/science-at-nasa/2009/23dec_voyager/

Ravilious, K. (2007, 2 28). *National Geographic News.* Retrieved from National Geographic: http://news.nationalgeographic.com/news/2007/02/070228-mars-warming.html

Rosenberg, M. (2015). *Non-Violent Communication.* Puddle Dancer Press: 3rd Edition.

Schucman, H. (2007). *A Course in Miracles - Combined Volume.* Mill Valley, CA: The Foundation for Inner Peace.

Tate, K. (2013). *How Quantum Entanglement Works. LiveScience Website: https://www.livescience.com/28550-how-quantum-entanglement-works-infographic.html*

Tellinger, M. (2012). *Ubuntu Movement.* Retrieved from Ubuntu Political Party, South Africa: www.ubuntuplanet.org

The Institute of Heart Math. (n.d.). *www.HeartMath.org*. Retrieved from www.heartmath.org/programs/emwave-self-regulation-technology-theoretical-basis/

Van Tassel, G. (1999). *The Council of 7 Lights*. Ministry of Universal Wisdom.

Wachowski, L. a. (Director). (1999). *The Matrix* [Motion Picture].

About the Author

Paige works intimately with empaths and awakening humans who need assistance activating their hearts and higher minds. She specializes in using a combination of talk-therapy and hypnotherapy for the healing of PTSD, relational and attachment trauma, betrayal, abandonment (from self or others), and inner child work. Confusion, depression, and anxiety are common among the awakening community. The resulting wreckage of "mis-attunement" from others creates lifetimes of loneliness for empaths and sensitive ones. She works to help individuals learn to recognize their own inner voice of truth. Her most recent field of study is the use of Universal Mind to trade the disempowerment of victimization for feelings of empowerment and bliss through remembering WHO WE REALLY ARE.

Paige has been a devoted student of Sufism since 1998, where she is ordained with the station of Sufi Master Teacher by the Shadhuliyya Higher Sufi Council. She is a long time spiritual seeker and practitioner, shamanic journey guide, certified hypnotherapist, intuitive empath, contactee, Volunteer Soul, and a passionate writer of transformational thought.

As a psychotherapist, mystic, healer, and psychic, Paige adores working one-on-one with individuals, as she also touches thousands through Zoom classes, YouTube lectures, and published works. She holds a Master's Degree in individual, and marriage and family therapy from St. Edward's University in Austin, and a clinical license to practice from the state of Texas. Her clinical training lies in the integration of somatic psychology with interpersonal neurobiology.

You can find Paige online at www.PaigeBartholomew.com. She runs a thriving, worldwide private practice via phone and internet, online group therapy for empaths and Volunteer Souls.

Her gift is in helping Awakening Ones remember who they truly are, and to heal blocks to Love. It is her highest honor to help shift the world from pain and confusion, into comfort and peace.

Learn More about Working One-On-One with Paige, Classes, and Zoom Groups
www.PaigeBartholomew.com

Follow Paige's "Love Revolution" on Facebook
by searching "Paige Bartholomew"

Made in the USA
Columbia, SC
03 August 2022

64483239R00167